Harriet Tubman

*A Captivating Guide to an American
Abolitionist Who Became the Most Famous
Conductor of the Underground Railroad*

Free Bonus from Captivating History (Available for a Limited time)

Hi History Lovers!

Now you have a chance to join our exclusive history list so you can get your first history ebook for free as well as discounts and a potential to get more history books for free! Simply visit the link below to join.

Captivatinghistory.com/ebook

Also, make sure to follow us on Facebook, Twitter and Youtube by searching for Captivating History.

Contents

Introduction: The Great Conductor

Harriet Tubman was known as a "conductor" on the "Underground Railroad." But this wasn't a railroad that carried trains and freight but rather human lives that were desperately seeking freedom. It was a clandestine group of individuals (hence the name "underground") scattered across the United States and Canada who helped facilitate the migration of those ensnared in the South's scourge of slavery to the so-called free states and provinces of the North.

No one knows exactly how this network began. But the first mention of the phrase appears in 1831 after an enslaved man from Kentucky ran away from his owner. The owner was recorded as saying that the man took an "underground road." There was then another reference in 1839 when a runaway slave was recaptured and, under duress, was forced to admit that he was trying to seek freedom by traveling down an "underground railroad to Boston."

At its height, the Underground Railroad consisted of a complex network of routes that stretched out into fourteen different Northern states. It is estimated that some 100,000 slaves found freedom by trusting its winding roads.

Those that chose to seek freedom through this underground network had to set out on a perilous course that would take them through woods, swamplands, rivers, and mountains while dodging any slave hunters that might be on their trail. It was conductors like Harriet Tubman that helped these brave souls navigate through this treacherous terrain. But as much as she aided slaves in their pursuit of freedom, she herself would not escape slavery's clutches unscathed.

Harriet's years of bondage were dreadful, and she had the scars to prove it. She also had recurring headaches from when a heavy two-pound weight used for weighing produce struck her in the head. Neither her scars nor her headaches would ever leave her, and they served as a constant reminder of what she had gone through. In fact, some biographies assert that as she got older, the headaches only grew worse.

But Harriet was a fighter. And she insisted on those around her having that same fighting spirit as well. Her steely determination was forged on the Underground Railroad, where to turn back meant slavery, severe punishment, and possibly death. Harriet Tubman traveled up and down the backroads in the dead of night, with only her own wits and her faith in God to help her.

It's said that at one point, Harriet began carrying a gun with her for her own personal protection. But the weapon also served as a deterrent in case anyone she "conducted" down the Underground Railroad might have second thoughts. On at least one occasion, one of her charges, exhausted and frightened, declared that they would be better off just turning around and going back to the plantation. Harriet didn't mince her words. She didn't give the person a pep talk to encourage them forward; she told them the truth. She knew the gravity of the situation better than anyone else—she knew that if even one person went back, they could talk, and by doing so, they could bring the whole operation down with them. As such, Harriet didn't pat the fearful doubter on the back and say, "There, there, it'll be alright." Nope. This woman pulled her gun on him and declared, "Dead folks tell no tales; you go on or die!"

Such strong-willed passion was enough to convince almost anyone that when they followed Harriet Tubman, they were in it for the long haul. Or, as she put it, "On my Underground Railroad, I never run my train off the track and I never lost a passenger." No matter what the cost, for anyone who entrusted themselves into her able hands, she was determined to see them through until the end.

Chapter 1 – Never Again

The woman that history recalls as Harriet Tubman was born with the name of Araminta Ross, and she was often referred to as simply "Minty." It was actually her mother who was first named Harriet—Harriet Araminta Green to be exact—and Tubman's father was a man named Benjamin Ross. Both of her parents were slaves. Although her exact birth date remains unknown, it is believed that she began life on a plantation in Maryland sometime around the year 1820.

The furthest Harriet Tubman's ancestry can be traced back is to her maternal grandmother, a woman called "Modesty," who originated from the so-called "Gold Coast" of West Africa. Although it's not known entirely for sure, it has been suggested that Harriet's family members in Africa were of the Ashanti tribe, a people group that still exists today in the West African nation of Ghana.

Slavery was by no means unknown to the Ashanti. Long before any Europeans arrived in their land, they themselves had a long history of enslaving each other and members of other tribes. Like many ancient African cultures, enslaving prisoners of war from rival tribes or even fellow tribesmen as punishment for alleged crimes was quite common. In some instances, it is said that the Ashanti even used their slaves as human sacrifices during their funeral rituals.

It's important to note, however, that the slavery practiced by the Ashanti had no racial component to it. One wasn't a slave simply because of how they looked; rather, it had to do with their social status. And despite the occasional horrid practice of human sacrifice, it is said that the Ashanti slaves were treated fairly well by their Ashanti masters, without the added ugliness of racism that was introduced during the European practice.

If Harriet Tubman's grandmother Modesty was indeed from the Ashanti tribe of West Africa, the year 2005 bore witness to a very special homecoming, for it was that year that two of Harriet's great-grandnieces paid a visit to their great-grand aunt's ancestral home. After tracing their roots to Tubman and then all the way back to Tubman's own aforementioned grandmother Modesty, who was ripped away from her African roots sometime in the 1700s, the trip brought some much-needed closure to the tragedy of the past.

Harriet was born about ten years after the War of 1812 started, which pitted a young America against the British just a few decades after the US had gained its formal independence from the British Crown. Harriet's native Maryland served a pivotal role in that conflict, with the Battle of Baltimore, which actually took place in 1814, being one of the most dramatic. The British navy had tried to force their way into the state but was beaten back by the American soldiers.

Of all of the veterans of the War of 1812, it was General Andrew Jackson who would come to be the most prominent in American life. Jackson was the territorial governor of the slavery stronghold of Florida in 1821, and he used this position, along with his popularity, to springboard himself into the presidential election of 1824. This first bid would fail, but Jackson would succeed the second time around, getting himself elected president in 1828.

Mr. Jackson, of course, is the man who ended up on the face of America's twenty-dollar bill, but recent legislation has since championed the idea of putting Harriet Tubman on the front of the bill and Andrew Jackson on the back. Many have noted the irony of having a slaveholding president, who was so far removed from the life and struggles of someone such as Harriet Tubman, sharing the same piece of currency with her.

When Andrew Jackson was president, Harriet Tubman was a little-known slave girl called "Minty" who worked and played in the fields of Maryland. Tubman herself wouldn't take the name of Harriet until later on in life, but since this is the name she has become most associated with, we will refer to her as such throughout this book for the sake of clarity.

Her parents actually came from two different plantations, so two separate slave-owning families are entangled with the story of their lives, and unraveling these family ties can be quite challenging. As one of Harriet Tubman's more recent biographers, Jean McMahon Humez, once explained, "The two white slaveholding families that controlled the lives of Tubman's parents and siblings intermarried, and the resulting 'blended family' relationships have bedeviled her biographers and are still confusing to explain." It is indeed difficult to unravel all of the complex dynamics that were at work in the lives of Harriet Tubman's family.

Nevertheless, let's attempt to break it down. Harriet Tubman's mother, who was also named Harriet, was originally owned by one Atthow Pattison. It was when Atthow Pattison died that she became the "property" of his granddaughter, Mary Pattison. Ms. Pattison then married a man named Joseph Brodess, who abruptly passed away a few years later. The couple had a son, meanwhile, by the name of Edward Brodess.

After the death of her first husband, Ms. Pattison Brodess remarried to a widower named Anthony Thompson, who lived nearby. Mr. Thompson already had a son at the time, who was named after his father and known as Anthony C. Thompson. Mr. Thompson was also the owner of Harriet Tubman's future father, Benjamin Ross.

It was from the union of these two plantation families that Benjamin Ross and Tubman's mother, Harriet Araminta Green, first met each other. And, of course, it was due to the union of Benjamin Ross and Harriet Araminta Green that the future Harriet Tubman came to be. Harriet was preceded by three sisters and a brother: Linah, Mariah, Soph, and Robert. Four more siblings, three brothers and a sister, would be born after Harriet, and they were Ben, Rachel, Henry, and Moses.

As much trauma as Harriet would eventually go through, her earliest days are said to have been surprisingly pleasant and carefree. Apparently, it was the nature of the plantation to have the smallest of children who were too young to work looked after by the slaves who were too old to work. In the first biography written about Tubman, *Scenes in the Life of Harriet Tubman*, this state of plantation affairs is vividly described. This piece speaks of how the slave children were free to play. But for those old enough to work the fields, listening to the children play made them "groan in spirit," knowing the horrible fate that would await these youngsters once they were deemed old and strong enough to work.

For Harriet, this coming of age into the brutal realities of slavery occurred when she was only five years old, for it was around that time that Mary Pattison Brodess "leased" Harriet out to do chores for others. It is indeed pretty horrible to imagine that a human being can be "leased" to another, but this was the sad state of affairs during Harriet's childhood. As rough as it was, she didn't know life could be any different. As we will see as we progress through this book, it was only when her eyes were finally opened to the possibilities that her spirit rose up in defiance to the bondage she was born into.

It was when she began working for others that she had begun to refer to herself by the nickname of Minty, as it was the habit of slaves to not want to give out their actual name when they shifted hands to different owners. At her new place of work, she was tasked with cleaning the house and babysitting.

Although she was still just a child, she was expected to work like an adult, and quite meticulously so. Harriet would later recall that her new mistress at this particular home, a pushy and authoritarian woman by the name of Mrs. Cook, would inspect the cleaning she did, and if she found any of Harriet's work unsatisfactory, she wouldn't hesitate to have Harriet "whipped about her face, neck, and back."

Often enough, her inability to perform certain tasks was simply due to a misunderstanding of what it was that she was being told to do. Instead of taking the time to properly explain to the child how to do things, her stern taskmasters typically resorted to just beating her instead. It was only when repeated whippings failed to bring better results that her cruel overseers realized that they needed to take the time to give her adequate instructions.

The damage was done, however, and due to this abuse, Harriet would carry permanent scars with her—both psychologically and physically—for the rest of her life. And to add insult to literal injury, when the woman who had worked Harriet within an inch of her life returned her to her previous owner, she complained that Harriet "hadn't been worth a penny."

Nevertheless, the complaining mistress would soon take Harriet back and would use her services as a babysitter. Harriet was made to tend to a baby that wasn't much smaller than herself. At night, she was expected to rock the infant while it slept, and if weary Harriet happened to nod off and fall asleep herself, she would be in a world of trouble, because as she fell asleep, the child would stir and cry like infants do, causing the mistress to come running and screaming at Harriet. If the baby so much as stirred in the middle of the night, Harriet would be threatened with the lash of her mistress's whip.

By contrast, her experience babysitting for her own mother was much more pleasant. Little Minty would often watch her younger siblings, usually with much relish. She would later recall:

> I used to be in a hurry for her [her mother] to go, so's I could play the baby was [pretend the baby was] a pig in a bag, and hold him up by the bottom of his dress. I had a nice frolic with that baby, swinging him all around his feet in the dress and his little head and arms touching the floor. Because I was too small to hold him higher. It was late nights before my mother got home, and when he'd get worrying, I'd cut a fat

chunk of pork and toast it on the coals and put it in his mouth. One night he went to sleep with that hanging out, and when my mother come home, she thought I'd done kill him. I nursed that there baby till he was so big I couldn't tote him any mo.

Here, from Harriet's own words, we can get a charming and amusing account of how she enjoyed taking care of and playing with her little brother. She would joke around with him and put him in a bag as if he were a little piggy just bought from the market. The child would giggle with glee and delight while Harriet swung him around just inches above the floor as if the baby was flying in the air.

Of course, her mother may not have always appreciated such roughhousing, but for little Harriet, this was joy in its purest form, and she did indeed have "a nice frolic with that baby." Such joyful misadventures with her siblings represented the few good memories she had of her youth. Even though her family was living in impoverished conditions and oppressed by the outside world, when they were together and allowed to simply be themselves, they enjoyed each other's company tremendously.

Besides cleaning and babysitting, another common chore Harriet was given when she was leased outside of the home was that of weaving. She didn't care too much for this kind of tedious work, however, and it certainly didn't help matters that her overseer, the aforementioned Mrs. Cook, was not exactly encouraging. It's said that Mrs. Cook always had an attitude with Harriet, and when the girl wasn't catching on to a task fast enough, she would viciously berate her, calling her "stupid and clumsy."

In light of these conditions, Harriet was grateful when the woman's husband, James Cook, came home one day with a new job for her. He had Harriet go outside so that she could keep an eye out on his muskrat traps. The muskrat is a small, furry, rodent-like creature that was prized in the South for both its fur and as a dietary supplement. Harriet felt much better being out in the open air, underneath the warmth of the sun, rather than having to endure the harsh words of her mistress while toiling under her icy stare.

Harriet didn't have anyone looking over her shoulder when she was outside tending the muskrat traps, as she was mostly left to her own accord. Even though she still wasn't yet free, the fact that Harriet was given this small amount of free agency meant everything to her. And, on some occasions, she even magnanimously extended that freedom to the very muskrats she caught. It's said that young Harriet would occasionally take pity on the critters and "set the animals free and watch them swim away." In many ways, this was her first taste of what freedom really meant.

As much as she enjoyed this reprieve from the harsh control of Mrs. Cook and her weaving, the swampy terrain where the muskrat traps were was not exactly the kind of place a youngster like Harriet should have been roaming about. The swamps were filled with bugs and other forms of pestilence that frequently made people sick. And soon enough, Harriet fell prey to a swamp-borne illness.

One day, she felt so terrible that she passed out in the swamps, causing her to be sent back to the care of her mother at her home plantation. This was, in some sense, a blessing in disguise, as it got her away from the tyrannical abuses of those she worked for and allowed her to recuperate in the loving embrace of her mother.

Her mother, as Tubman would later recall, was actually quite skilled in herbal remedies for just about any form of sickness. This was a skill that would serve Harriet Tubman well, as her mother helped her recover from various episodes of fever, flu, colds, and the like. Not willing to deal with a slave that was frequently sick and unavailable for work, the Cooks gave up on Harriet altogether.

It wasn't long, however, before she was sent to another woman, a certain Miss Susan, who was in need of someone to do some babysitting and general chores around the house. This tyrannical micromanager did not find Harriet's work to be satisfactory, and she received routine beatings for failing to live up to her mistress's demands. Harriet was often left hungry and deprived, and as she later recalled, she was so famished that one day she stole a sugar cube that was left out in the open.

Miss Susan saw her, and Harriet, realizing she would get a bad beating for her actions, fled the scene and hid in a pigsty for several days, subsisting on the scraps that were thrown to the pigs. In many ways—whether she realized it or not—this impulsive flight from Miss Susan's whip was her very first attempt to take charge and flee for her freedom. But she couldn't hide in a pigsty forever, of course. Eventually, she would have to go back.

And sadly enough, she was indeed punished, not just for eating the sugar cube but for running away, and she was given a terrible beating as a consequence. She was beaten so badly, in fact, that it is said she suffered from "internal injuries." In the aftermath, even the tyrannical Miss Susan realized that Harriet wouldn't be able to work in such a condition, and so, Harriet was sent back to the Brodess household from which she had come.

Harriet, like any slave, obviously had a hard life, but for those on the outside, they often questioned why she was so "moody." Even after all she had been through, it was still suggested that she was a listless and chronic malcontent. It's hard for us to imagine in modern times how anyone forced to live under such conditions could be cheerful, but apparently, her owners and taskmasters took umbrage to what they deemed as an ornery and "bad attitude."

Perhaps Harriet was just not willing to be anyone's slave. She didn't quite know what freedom was, yet something deep inside of her knew that the condition that she was in was wrong. She felt the wrongness of it deep in the bottom of her soul, and in her mind, she was actively seeking a remedy. One thing that she knew for certain was that she did not like being cooped up in the house under the constant watch of a taskmaster.

Her owner soon realized this, and as such, he began to have her working in the field outside by the time she was entering adolescence. Here, Harriet could once again feel the wind on her face and the warmth of the sun on her skin, and she could at least imagine what it was like to be free. It was also here with the other field workers that she first heard mention of the mysterious Underground Railroad.

She was kept around in the field because she proved to be a good worker when it came to the hard farm work of planting and collecting crops. This work was also pivotal in strengthening Harriet's small physique, which would prove invaluable in her eventual march to freedom. She learned from her fellow field workers that it was possible to find freedom simply by taking note of the position of certain stars in the sky, such as the Big Dipper and Polaris, more commonly known as the North Star.

This revelation set the wheels of freedom in motion. But she wasn't ready to act just yet. The catalyst that would send her over the edge was when her owner ran into money problems and sold her two elder siblings, Soph and Linah. From this point on, these two sisters completely vanished from Harriet's life. But she would never forget them. And the memory of being forcibly separated from these family members would burn itself into her memory and have a steadfast and determined Harriet Tubman quietly tell herself, "never again."

Chapter 2 – Harriet's Vision Begins to Take Shape

Of all the evils of slavery, one of the worst aspects of the whole terrible enterprise was the fact that any slave could be separated from their family at a moment's notice. If a slave owner thought that they could make a profit by parting ways with a slave or, as was the case when Harriet was a child, by simply leasing them out to another individual, they wouldn't hesitate to do so.

Even though slaves, like Harriet's parents, considered themselves to be married, there was no legal binding between slave family members, and as such, they could be torn from each other at any time. The fact that an outside force could interfere with a family unit in such a way made some slaves hesitant to even get married in the first place. Yet slave unions still persisted, with couples trying their best to mitigate the hardship and uncertainty that they faced.

In comparison with other slaves, Harriet was blessed to have both parents and her siblings together under the same roof. But at a young age, the familial rug was pulled out from under her when her two elder sisters, Soph and Linah, were ripped apart from her family. Harriet's owner, Edward Brodess, was facing some tough financial circumstances, and in order to recoup his losses, he resorted to selling human collateral.

As horrific as it all is, Edward sold Harriet's sisters just to pay off his mounting debts. Making matters even worse was the fact that Soph and Linah had children of their own that they were forced to leave behind. Harriet was there to see the anguish of both her mother, as well as Soph's and Linah's children, as they all cried in sorrow, not knowing what might become of Soph and Linah. In one fell swoop, Brodess had torn a family completely asunder just to pay some miscellaneous bills that he owed.

The idea that your loved ones could suddenly be sold to a plantation farther south was a constant reminder of just how precarious the life of a slave could be. Many are not aware of it, but it's from this traumatic experience that the popular American expression of being "sold down the river" comes from. The expression originated from the days of slavery when slaves of the Upper South, such as in Maryland, lived under the constant threat of being sold farther "down the Mississippi River" to the much harsher conditions of the Deep South.

Although none of the sources seem to be clear on the date, it is said that sometime after Harriet's sisters were sold, Harriet's mother put her foot down and would not allow any of her remaining children to be taken from her. It's hard to imagine what someone in her condition could do, but according to a story later related by Tubman's brother Henry, she was so desperate to keep her children that this fearless woman was ready to pull out all the stops in order to prevent another painful separation.

According to Harriet's brother Henry, one day, a man from Georgia came around the Maryland plantation seeking to buy slaves. After speaking with Harriet Ross's (Harriet Tubman's mother) owner, he apparently agreed to buy Ms. Ross's youngest son, Moses. But the child's mother apparently knew what was afoot, and she confronted her owner. She left her work in the field and heard him negotiating with the "Georgia man," with her owner telling the stranger, "I ought to have fifty dollars more yet." Apparently, her owner was not quite satisfied with how much the "Georgia man" planned on bidding in the purchase of little Moses and was telling him that he "ought to have fifty dollars more" for the sale. It was right in the middle of all this haggling that Harriet's mom burst onto the scene, demanding, "What do you want of the boy?"

Caught off guard, her owner sought some way to get her out of sight, and without answering, he ordered her to "Go and bring a pitcher of water." Harriet did as she was requested and then went back to the fields. But shortly thereafter, the plantation owner began calling for Moses. Instead of letting Moses answer the call, Harriet's mother popped up, once again demanding to know what her owner wanted with her son.

The owner, indignant at the intrusion, shouted, "What did you come for? I hollered for the boy?" Harriet's mother then declared in no uncertain terms that her son was "not for sale" and that if anyone came looking for him, they would get their skull broke in two. It's pretty amazing that a slave could stand up to their master like this, but Ms. Ross was desperate not to lose her little boy, and she made her owner realize that she had reached her breaking point.

Still, the owner persisted, but Ms. Ross had actually hidden Moses in the remote swamps south of the plantation, and when the plantation owner and the slave trader came looking for the boy, they were disappointed. A harsher master might have pushed the matter further, but her owner quickly decided such a confrontation would be more trouble than it was worth and simply let the matter drop. This incident—if it happened as described—would have served as a valuable lesson to Harriet Tubman that defiance was indeed possible.

This idea was further cemented by some of the stories that young Harriet heard from other slaves while she was working in the field. It was in 1831, when she was around eleven years of age, that she heard one of the most startling of these tales, for it was around this time that news was trickling through the community that there had been a massive uprising of slaves at a plantation some one hundred miles from where Harriet was.

In that year, a slave named Nat Turner launched a rebellion of some sixty slaves at a plantation in Virginia, which resulted in the deaths of fifty white Southerners. Nat Turner's rebellion was eventually put down, but the very idea that slaves could take matters into their own hands and rise up against their masters in such a dramatic fashion put both a lasting fear in the hearts of slave owners and a kernel of hope in the hearts of those held in bondage.

Nevertheless, it was with a pall of gloom hanging over them that Harriet and her family spent much of the early 1830s. As worried slaveholders began to tighten the constraints that held the slaves bound—both literally and metaphorically—their conditions would soon become even more difficult than usual.

Unsure of what might happen, Harriet just kept one foot in front of the other as she continued to work the fields. It was in this manner that she was busying herself in the harvest year of 1835 that Harriet's attention was suddenly drawn to a slave by the name of Jim, as he suddenly stood up from his work and took off. Harriet stared in confusion as she saw him dart across the field. Where was he going? What was he doing? Was this going to be another Nat Turner's rebellion in the making?

The overseer, Mr. McCracken, knew exactly what Jim was doing, however, and immediately chased after him. Not sure what else to do, Harriet followed the overseer to see what was happening. She trailed behind as McCracken chased Jim all the way to a local general store. There are actually a few versions of what transpired next, but the most repeated one seems to indicate that Jim was hiding out in the back of the store when McCracken went inside.

Jim then tried to get past McCracken. Mr. McCracken saw Harriet standing in the doorway and asked for her help, telling her to block the door so Jim couldn't get away. But instead of blocking the exit, she stepped to the side and let Jim out. She then proceeded to block the door so that the overseer wouldn't be able to chase after Jim. Some accounts say that, in his anger, McCracken took a "two-pound weight" from a brass scale that was used to weigh produce and purposefully threw it at Harriet. However, other accounts say that he hit her by accident and was actually trying to hit Jim with it as he ran out the door.

At any rate, Harriet was somehow struck in the head that day, and she was left seriously injured. She was hit so hard, in fact, that it cracked her cranium. She was in rough shape, and even the cruel overseer knew that she needed immediate attention and took her to get help. But, as Harriet recalled, the "help" she received was virtually non-existent.

As she later remembered, "They carried me to the house all bleeding and fainting. I had no bed, no place to lie down on at all, and they lay me on the seat of the loom, and I stayed there all that day and next, and the next day I went to work again and there I worked with the blood and sweat rolling down my face till I couldn't see."

It remains unclear if there was any exaggeration on Harriet's part when it came to the immediate aftermath of the blow she received. The injury most certainly was severe, but Harriet claimed that she was forced to get right back to work the very next day, forced to toil with "blood and sweat rolling down" her cheeks. Other biographers insist that Harriet was completely knocked out and "in a coma for weeks, lying on a bed of rags in the corner of her family's windowless wooden cabin."

Whatever the case may be, her frantic mother most certainly tried to do whatever was in her power to nurse her ailing daughter back to health. Since slaves were not allowed regular medical care, this meant that much of Harriet's treatment involved whatever natural remedies that other slaves could make use of. Fortunately for Harriet, her mother was said to have been a skilled herbalist and healer, and through the time-tested methods of her ancestral lore, she was at least able to ease Harriet's suffering.

This was no small task, though, as Harriet most likely was suffering from a severe concussion, if not a fractured skull. She would have a distinct scar from where she was struck and even a visible indentation on her forehead. But these marks were not the only lasting effect that the incident would leave upon Harriet.

According to later accounts, Harriet was beset with fits of "unconsciousness," seemingly falling into a deep sleep out of nowhere. It has been said that Harriet could suddenly pass out without warning, losing consciousness several times a day, and "nothing could rouse her." Apparently, even the lash of the overseer couldn't wake her up once she was out.

Unsure of what to do, the very overseer that had struck her began to consult with others about selling Harriet since the difficulties she was experiencing was making her unproductive. For her owners, Harriet was more or less just damaged goods, and soon enough, they began considering selling her just to get the burden off their hands.

But, of course, no one was too eager to buy a slave that was sick all the time and unable to work. Harriet herself later described the situation when she recalled, "They wouldn't give a sixpence for me." So it was that Harriet Tubman found herself in a kind of slavery limbo.

Nevertheless, with the able hands of her mother, she was eventually able to recover enough to get back to work. Her next immediate overseer was a man named John T. Stewart, whom she began working for in 1836. Stewart was a shipbuilder, and he was known as something of a "local entrepreneur." He had set to work several African Americans, both free and slave alike, on a lumber project he had been cultivating for several years.

Harriet, however, was initially sent to work in Stewart's home as a domestic servant, but Tubman had long since developed a decided distaste for housework and asked Stewart if she could work out at the lumberyard with the men instead. Stewart must have hesitated at first, knowing that such heavy industry was typically reserved for male slaves, and considering the fact that she had only just recently recovered from a serious injury, Stewart must have doubted the wisdom of placing her in such an intense environment. However, Harriet persisted, and he eventually granted her wish.

Placed out on the lumberyard, her work entailed of the cutting and hauling of lumber for the bustling shipyards of Baltimore, Maryland. Stewart would not be disappointed in his decision. Harriet quickly proved herself to be a hard worker, and it is said she was able to hold her own with the best of them.

Among those that worked for Mr. Stewart was Harriet Tubman's own father, Benjamin Ross. Benjamin's original owner had actually died that very year, making his son, Dr. Anthony Thompson, his owner. The elder Thompson's will stipulated that Benjamin Ross should be freed by the time he turned 45. Ben would reach this milestone four years later in 1840, and Dr. Thompson would indeed fulfill his father's wishes and grant Harriet's dad his freedom.

It must have been a bittersweet moment for Benjamin Ross. Surely, he was happy to have finally gained his freedom. But, at the same time, he must have looked at his own wife and children with anguish, knowing that they were still firmly ensnared in the terrible bondage of slavery. The moment of Benjamin's emancipation could be regarded as one of the seminal events that spurred both Benjamin and Harriet to contemplate freedom for the rest of the family.

In the meantime, during his last few years of bondage, Benjamin had shown quite a bit of promise working for Stewart, and due to both his industriousness and ingenuity, he had been made a "timber inspector." In this role, he was in charge of several people as they chopped down trees and carried away lumber. Harriet, too, enjoyed working for her father, and when she did so, she would chop down trees with the best of them, as well as "split rails" and "haul logs." She was, in fact, said to carry about "half a cord of wood a day." Mr. Stewart himself would boast that Harriet was so strong that "she could lift a barrel filled with produce, or pull a plow just like an ox could."

Back at her home plantation, Harriet's owner, Edward Brodess, was well pleased too. He was so impressed with her work, in fact, that Harriet was allowed to keep some of the money she made for him.

Eventually, she was able to save up enough to buy her own oxen, which she then used to aid her in her work even further so that she could earn even more money. Just like her father, Harriet Tubman was quite industrious and resourceful.

But there was more to Harriet Tubman than just her labor. What most would never have suspected when looking upon her stoic countenance were the fantastic visions that were taking place in her mind's eye. Later in life, Harriet would reveal that ever since the day that McCracken's wrath caused her to suffer that awful head injury, she had incredible dreams and visions.

Her father would later verify these flights of fancy and claim that Harriet had been able to predict everything from the weather to the outbreak of the Mexican-American War in 1846! As she grew older, Harriet would become quite religious. At this point, her dreams and visions began to take on new meanings for her. Soon, she began to view them as nothing short of direct messages from God.

Anyone who got to know Harriet quickly realized how important this mystical side was. Her later biographer Sarah Bradford described Harriet as thus: "She is the most shrewd and practical person in the world, yet she is a firm believer in omens, dreams and warnings. She declares that before her escape from slavery, she used to dream of flying over fields and towns, and rivers and mountains, looking down upon them 'like a bird.'"

Dreams of flying actually aren't all that uncommon. There are quite a few of us that may have had a dream like this from time to time. But for Harriet, such things held more meaning. For in those nighttime journeys across fields and meadows, she was doing more than just dreaming and fantasizing; she was plotting a course. While she was still in bondage, she envisioned herself soaring above it all like an eagle. And one day soon, she would make those dreams a reality.

Chapter 3 – Harriet Makes a Break for Freedom

The early 1840s were pivotal years for Harriet Tubman. Her father had been freed, and she had since gone back to her old owner. Since the children of female slaves were always the property of their mother's owner, this meant that the Brodess family remained in control of Harriet, her mother, and all of her siblings, even though her father had been freed by Dr. Thompson. Still, Harriet and her family had hope that one day their freedom would come as well.

Shortly after her father's emancipation, Harriet met a free black man by the name of John Tubman. It is said that John was actually born free, as his parents had already gained their freedom by the time of his birth. Such things were becoming increasingly common in Maryland at the time, as it was a state that boasted a fairly large population of African Americans, of whom nearly half were indeed considered free at the time.

It was through her marriage to John Tubman that Harriet acquired the last name that she would become so famous for. It is believed that Harriet and John Tubman were married to each other in the year 1844. But other than the name of her spouse and the year they were wed, it must be stressed that relatively little is known of exactly how this union came about, although it is suggested that they must have met during the time that Harriet was in the employment of John Stewart.

As mentioned, John already had a free status, so this allowed him to live wherever he chose. Harriet, on the other hand, was still beholden to whoever she was laboring under. This meant that John most likely had to make his living arrangements match Harriet's just so he could be close to her. It certainly would have been a tenuous and stressful arrangement for husband and wife, for sure.

We don't know a whole lot about the personal dynamics between Harriet and her husband John. It's been said that while Harriet was reserved, John could be arrogant and downright "haughty" at times. He was also older than Harriet, as evidenced by the lone photograph of the couple, which shows a young Harriet Tubman standing next to a seated, grey-bearded John Tubman.

It was shortly after Harriet's marriage to John Tubman that she decided to look into her own family history a bit. She hired a lawyer to look into the will of her mother's former owner, Atthow Pattison. As mentioned earlier in this book, Atthow Pattison was the previous owner of Harriet's mother, before she passed into the Brodess family by virtue of Mary Pattison marrying Joseph Brodess.

The attorney made a startling discovery. According to the will that Atthow Pattison left behind, Mary Pattison was supposed to set Harriet's mother free by the time she reached 45 years of age. But instead of fulfilling the terms of Atthow's will, Mary had simply ignored them altogether, and she instead passed Harriet's mother on to Edward Brodess when she should have already been freed. Harriet was infuriated to learn of these duplicitous dealings, and it quickened her resolve to figure out a way to free herself and her family on her own.

Shortly thereafter, tremendous fuel was added to this fire when Harriet learned that her current owner, Edward Brodess, intended to sell both her and her brothers off to a "chain gang to the far south." As bad as conditions may have been in Maryland, she knew from the stories she had heard among other slaves that the situation in the Deep South was even worse. She likely wouldn't have wanted her husband John to follow her to such a hostile place, even if he wanted to.

As part of a chain gang, she would be forced to pick cotton under the boiling heat of the sun all day long. For Harriet, such toiling, monotonous work would be far worse than simply hauling heavy lumber and other loads like she had been used to doing. She knew that in the cotton fields, speed was valued more than strength, and if anyone were to fall behind, they would soon face the lash of the overseer's whip. She knew that with her personal afflictions—her periodic headaches and fatigue—she would not be able to last very long in such a high-pressure environment.

Worried about what may happen to her, she turned to God. Harriet, although unable to read the Bible, was brought up by two very religious parents, and she had inherited her sense of spirituality from them. With no other recourse, she decided to take her case to God, praying with all of her heart that her owner would change his mind. As Harriet would later recall, she prayed for "the dear Lord to change that man's heart and make him a Christian."

She did this in her desire for him to become a more compassionate soul, who wouldn't cast her to the side so easily. But in the coming days before her impending auction, when she realized that he wasn't going to change, she became angry. And out of her frustrated desperation, instead of asking God to change Brodess, she asked for him to strike him dead! As Harriet would later relate, she began to pray, "Lord, if you ain't never going to change that man's heart, kill him, Lord, and take him out of the way, so he won't do no more mischief."

Strangely enough, her prayer would be answered. Shortly afterward, on March 7th, 1849, Edward Brodess would indeed pass away. Many will probably assume that this was actually just a coincidence, but Harriet felt personally responsible and immediately repented of her prayer. As she related to Sarah Bradford many years after the fact, "I would give the world full of silver and gold, if I had it, to bring that poor soul back. I would give myself; I would give everything! But he was gone, I couldn't pray for him no more."

Besides the guilt that she may have felt, the demise of her former owner didn't change her impending sale. His passing only forestalled Harriet's problems because once he was gone, it was his wife, Elizabeth Ann Brodess, that would take over and continue the plans of her late husband, right where he left off. And it was very much Elizabeth's intention to sell Harriet to a plantation in the Deep South, just as she had feared.

Under the stress of considering what her future might hold, Harriet once again began to have powerful visions that she would attempt to interpret. One of these vivid dreams frightened her more than the others, in which she visualized a chaotic scene of men on horseback descending upon the slave quarters and grabbing hold of slaves, separating them from their families. She would often arise from such a dream in tears, sobbing out loud, "Oh, they're coming, they're coming. I must go."

She tried to share some of her doubts and fears with her husband John, but he wouldn't listen to her. He even went so far as to say that her "visions" were simply "proof" that her "dull witted" brain wasn't "thinking clearly." And when she confided in him about her conviction that she needed to leave, he actually threatened to report her to her owner if she didn't stop talking about it. Their relationship became rocky after this, to say the least, and John kept a wary eye on her lest she should suddenly take off.

Nevertheless, whether her husband supported her or not, she set about planning her escape regardless. Harriet's first effort to flee occurred in the fall of 1849. In this exodus, she managed to take two of her brothers with her, who were working at a nearby plantation. Since her husband's passing, their current owner, "Mistress Eliza Brodess," was having a hard time keeping up with just how many slaves she had and who worked where.

Harriet sought to take advantage of this confusion. And the fact that it would take a while for Eliza to even know that they had left would give them a valuable head start. They also made sure to leave on a Saturday night since slaves typically did not work on Sunday, and as such, their absence would not seem amiss.

Nevertheless, once Eliza realized what had happened, she sent out the alert and posted a cash reward for anyone who might bring the runaways back to the plantation. Although Harriet was resolute in her desire to make a break for freedom, her brothers began to have second thoughts. The trip north suddenly seemed altogether unfamiliar and frightening. And every step they took, her brothers began to fear the consequences should they be captured as runaways.

It was as if this fear completely overwhelmed them, for they eventually told Harriet that they could go no farther. With great hesitation, she listened to her brothers, and all three of them returned back to the plantation. But although her brothers had given up on the idea of making a break for it, Harriet was still convinced that she needed to somehow find her way to freedom.

This first attempt was, in many ways, her dress rehearsal. Taking all of this into consideration, she steeled her nerves and prepared herself to make an escape all by herself. According to her later recollection, she secretly alerted those near and dear to her of her intentions by singing a religious song, whose personal meaning they could not have mistaken.

Walking around one night outside of the slave's quarters, she sang, "I'm sorry friends, to leave you, farewell! Oh, farewell! But I'll meet you in the morning, farewell! Oh, farewell!" As the sad, wistful melody continued to build, she then ended with the refrain, "I'll meet you in the morning, when you reach the promised land. On the other side of Jordan, for I'm bound for the promised land!"

Among those listening was Harriet Tubman's niece, Mary Ann, who understood exactly what Harriet had in mind. And being privy to this knowledge, she filled in Harriet's parents and siblings of what was transpiring as soon as it was prudent to do so. Most of those close to

Harriet kept her disappearance secret, but her husband did not. John Tubman actually informed Eliza of Harriet's departure as soon as he realized she was gone.

John Tubman has long been vilified for this, but just to play the devil's advocate here, let's try to see things from his perspective. He knew that the journey that Harriet was attempting to undertake would put her in grave danger. The chances of her succeeding were very slim, and the chances of her taking a wrong turn and getting lost were very great. John Tubman had no idea at the time that Harriet would prove to be such a superb navigator. She had sustained a head injury as a child after all, and she suffered from lifelong ailments because of it.

Having said that, it could be that he—albeit in a way that's hard for us to fathom today—believed that he had Harriet's best interests at heart. If he felt that her flight would only bring her to ruin, then maybe he was trying to do what he thought was best for her. Also, he could very well have been saving up money to purchase her freedom himself. Such things were not uncommon.

And one does indeed have to wonder why a free man would marry a slave unless he had plans to somehow free her eventually. Even if she was sold farther downriver, if John truly loved Harriet, he could have moved to be near her new place of employment and find a way to keep in contact with her. On the other hand, however, John Tubman could have been just as nefarious as later biographers made him out to be.

According to Tubman biographer Sarah Bradford, John mercilessly teased her and insinuated that she was dimwitted and slow in the head because of her previous injury. It's said that John Tubman was mean to Harriet, "called her fool, and said she was like old Cudjo, who, when a joke went round, never laughed till half an hour after everybody else got through." In other words, he was trying to say that she was so dumb that she didn't get the punchline of a joke until a half-hour later, after everyone had already laughed and it wasn't even funny anymore. This is obviously not a very endearing thing for a husband to say to his wife. If John really was this toxic and cruel of a character as Bradford suggests, then perhaps the only reason he didn't want Harriet to run away was that he didn't want to lose his control over her.

Many domineering spouses who verbally abuse their partner do so to make them feel small and insignificant so that they can better dominate them. If that's the case, maybe John liked things just the way they were, and he feared Harriet gaining her freedom just as much as her master did. It's a frightening thing to speculate.

But without any further historical records, just about all we know about Harriet's first marriage to John Tubman is pure speculation. Nevertheless, whether she was running from the oppression of slavery or an overbearing, oppressive husband, Harriet Tubman was determined to gain her freedom.

Chapter 4 – First Forays on the Underground Railroad

Harriet's trek north wasn't easy, but fortunately, she had a little help along the way. One of the first accounts of her journey tells us that shortly before she made her escape, she had befriended a white woman—a practitioner of the Quaker faith—who promised to help her if she needed anything. Not a whole lot is known about this mysterious figure, but it seems that she lived somewhere close enough to serve as the first way station on Harriet Tubman's journey north.

The Quakers, as a whole, were adamantly against slavery and had made several collective efforts to stem the tide of it. It was an official part of the Quaker dogma early on that slavery was to be viewed as an evil practice and that they should do everything possible to alleviate those who were in bondage. Having said that, it wouldn't be at all surprising that a Quaker would aid a runaway slave like Harriet.

According to this account, her Quaker contact gave her a "piece of paper with two names on it," which were actually further contacts she could reach out to for aid as she made her way north. Harriet, of course, couldn't read it—like most slaves, she had never been taught—but she was verbally instructed on how to find where these contacts were located.

When she arrived at the home of the first contact, a woman answered the door. Harriet showed her the scrap of paper she carried, and the lady immediately recognized Harriet's plight. Feeling sorry for her, this first contact gave her a quick bite to eat, but lest they attract the undue attention of her neighbors, she instructed Harriet to pretend that she was there to work and had her sweep the steps to the house and the surrounding yard outside.

This subterfuge was very much necessary since it was considered a grave criminal offense for anyone to aid in the escape of a slave. And if suspicious neighbors were alerted to what was going on, they could have reported what was happening and brought trouble down on all who were involved. So it was that Harriet carried out this charade until the woman's husband came home, for it was the husband who would be crucial for the next leg of Harriet's journey.

Upon his arrival, this man assisted Harriet into the back of a covered wagon and then drove her to the next town over. Letting her out of the wagon, Harriet was then directed to follow the Choptank River that went toward Delaware, which would ultimately lead her to the free state of Pennsylvania. During this perilous exodus, Harriet moved by night and kept out of sight during the day so she wouldn't be detected.

Another reason that she moved by night was so that she could follow the North Star. The North Star—that bright celestial object near the Big Dipper, or, as many of the slaves called it, "the Drinking Gourd"—is a great way for any traveler to make sure they are moving north. But some contend that the Drinking Gourd was of more importance to runaway slaves such as Harriet Tubman than has previously been disclosed.

A more recent—albeit highly controversial—book, written by a self-proclaimed "witch doctor" who goes by the name of "Utu," has put forth the claim that Tubman routinely mixed Christianity with aspects of African ancestral religion. Such things wouldn't be unheard of, and anyone who goes down to the Creole South or the Caribbean can see evident mixtures of Christianity and African lore. In such places, it isn't uncommon to see a Voodoo priestess praying over a statue of the Virgin Mary.

Utu refers to the celestial bodies that Tubman followed as being the "Drinking Gourd and North Star Doorway." According to Utu, the "North Star was sung to and wished upon as the great navigator." The slaves who toiled in the fields looked up to this "doorway" as their gateway to freedom. Utu calls Tubman a "conjurer" and claims that the North Star was a very mystical thing for her. Utu claims that Tubman would focus on the North Star, knowing full well that it can "reflect back to us that which was conjured into it."

At any rate, whatever significance the North Star may have had, Harriet was in for an arduous trek. It has been estimated that her trip north may have taken as long as two weeks. Even though she had some help along the way, the idea that she was able to make such a demanding journey by herself across such uncertain terrain was remarkable, to say the least.

The sheer loneliness of traveling through the wilderness for several days would have been too much for most people—as was the case of Harriet's own brothers—but Harriet always claimed that she felt a "divine presence" that guided her and kept her company at all times. And by the time she arrived in the freedom of the North, she felt as if she were in heaven. As Harriet described that fateful moment, "I looked at my hands to see if I was the same person now [that] I was free. There was such a glory over everything, the sun came like gold through the trees, and over the fields, and I felt like I was in heaven."

Upon her arrival in Pennsylvania, Tubman was introduced to the leading abolitionists in the city. These new and trusted friends of Harriet's helped her to find work and a place to stay. One of the most influential people that she came into contact with during this period was an African American activist by the name of William Still. Mr. Still was a clerk at the Pennsylvania Anti-Slavery Society in Philadelphia, an organization that made it their mission to help runaway slaves like Harriet.

In many ways, Mr. Still was the gateway that all of the brave souls who made the journey north passed through, with him meticulously taking down their names and as many other identifying characteristics as possible. He did this not only because he wanted to get to know those who escaped but also as a means of later being able to reunite freed slaves with their family members that they had left behind. This aspect of Still's records would be very important for Harriet herself, for as soon as she arrived in the North, she began contemplating how to bring as many of her relatives as she could back with her.

After her arrival in Philadelphia, she found work and lodging, and she was as self-sufficient as ever, but she also realized that she often felt isolated, alienated, and alone. She had made some new friends in the North for sure, but she was still in a land that was largely foreign to her, and as bad as the South had been, she missed some of the people she knew and the times they had together.

Harriet herself would later explain her feelings.

> I had crossed the line of which I had so long been dreaming. I was free; but there was no one to welcome me to the land of freedom, I was a stranger in a strange land, and my home after all was down in the old cabin quarter, with the old folks, and my brothers and sisters. But to this solemn resolution I came; I was free, and they should be free also; I would make a home for them in the North, and the Lord helping me, I would bring them all there.

Harriet desperately longed for the people that she knew and loved. She knew that she would never willingly go back to the plantation, so she decided that she would bring them to her. Aiding her in this endeavor were contacts like William Still, who was able to get information from new arrivals about what was going on in her old home state of Maryland. She also sought the aid of abolitionists who could read so that they could relate to her the important information in the newspapers, especially those sections that detailed the movement and selling of slaves.

It was through this pipeline of information that Harriet managed to do enough detective work to figure out that her beloved niece, Mary Ann (sometimes also called Keziah) Bowley, was at a plantation in Baltimore. Harriet then formulated a plot to go and rescue her niece.

Her niece Mary Ann was actually in a similar situation as she had been; she was an enslaved woman married to a free African American. She and her two children were also on the verge of being auctioned off to another plantation, thereby severing yet another family. In Harriet's efforts to save her, she reached out to Mary's husband, John Bowley, first. She had one of her literate friends write Mr. Bowley a letter.

It was in this missive that Harriet advised John that she could "conduct" Mary's safe passage from Baltimore to Philadelphia, but she needed his help first. John Bowley must have been surprised to hear from Harriet, to say the least, but unlike Harriet's former husband, he readily agreed to help set his wife free. So, when Mary was placed on the auction block in December of 1850, John Bowley put Harriet's plan into motion.

It was a masterful scheme of subterfuge that had Mary's own husband make the winning bid on his wife. Such things were actually fairly common. It wasn't at all unusual for a free black man like John Bowley to save up money and use it to purchase the freedom of his other family members. So, when John showed up and began placing his bid, no one questioned him.

His wife's kids stood on the auction block as the bidding price went higher and higher. Once the price was high enough to meet the demands of the seller, the winning bid was declared, and it was none other than John Bowley. It's at this point that the auctioneer who was handling the bids "called a recess." The auctioneer then announced that he would return shortly after grabbing a bite to eat.

While the auctioneer was out taking his lunch break, John Bowley went into action. He walked right up to his wife and kids and walked them out of the courtroom. Amazingly enough, no one questioned him; he was, after all, the man who made the winning bid. And as prejudiced as some slaveholding Southerners could be, the color of green always bought respect.

The thing is, however, even though John had placed the winning bid, he hadn't yet actually put down any money for the purchase. He would have had to wait for the auctioneer to return in order to make it official. But John Bowley wasn't about to wait around for that. He never had any intention of actually paying for the bid; it was all just a means to distract those in attendance long enough to allow Mary and her kids to escape.

When the auctioneer returned, he called for Bowley, the winning bidder, to come forward, but, of course, by then, he and his wife and children were already long gone. As soon as the auctioneer realized he had been duped, a search for the Bowley family was launched. John Bowley, his wife Mary, and their children, meanwhile, hid in a safe house nearby until the coast was clear.

Later that evening, John took his family to the harbor, loaded them up in a boat, and sailed all the way to Baltimore. Here they met up with Harriet Tubman, who had been hiding out at Bowley's Baltimore residence. Harriet Tubman then helped guide the whole family back to Philadelphia, Pennsylvania, with her.

Of the family members she rescued, she would develop a close relationship with her nephew James Bowley. She eventually paid for his schooling, paving the way for James Bowley to one day become a successful school teacher. He was so successful, in fact, that after the end of the Civil War, he went back to the South to teach the recently emancipated slaves.

Shortly after this successful recovery, Harriet Tubman is said to have rescued "a brother and two other men." It has been suggested that this involved the rescue of her brother Moses. But not all sources make mention of this trip, and so, the details remain unclear. It was the excursion she made to Maryland in the autumn of 1851, however, that stands out the most. For it was on this mission that Harriet would attempt to recover the husband she had been estranged with ever since she made her flight north in 1849.

Harriet knew that her husband had not been supportive of her and had even tried to get her in trouble with her former owner in the past, but all the same, she still desired to reunite with the man she thought she loved. It's said that she even bought him a brand-new suit for the occasion. But sadly, all of her efforts would end with bitter despair when she discovered that he had since remarried to another woman.

Adding insult to injury, the two even proceeded to laugh at her when, out of the kindness of her heart, she offered to help both John and his new wife gain safe passage to the North. But rather than an ending, in many ways, the severance from her husband was a beginning. Because instead of bringing back the one man she thought she needed to settle down in a quiet life in the North, she instead became emboldened to make many more trips up and down the Underground Railroad to bring countless others to freedom.

Chapter 5 – General Tubman Takes Charge

As far as the movement to abolish slavery within the United States had come, it had taken several steps back in the year 1850, as this was the year that marked the passage of the Fugitive Slave Act. This piece of legislation mandated that anyone of African descent who was even merely "suspected" of being a fugitive—in other words, those slaves who were on the run—could be immediately hauled off to jail. This suddenly put any African American—even those who had been free their entire lives—in jeopardy.

It was certainly a precarious condition to be in. At any moment, a nosy neighbor or even just a hostile passerby could accuse you of being a fugitive slave and have you placed behind bars or hauled off to a plantation somewhere. It was this sense of having the rug pulled out from under them that led many freed slaves to seek refuge even farther north—as far north as Canada, in fact.

In Canada, things were completely different. Slavery had been made illegal in 1834, so it was actually a crime to make someone a slave. As such, there was no such thing as "fugitive slaves" in Canada. This is why Canada became such an attractive option for many former slaves, including Harriet Tubman. Leading so many through the wilderness was obviously no easy task, but Harriet was ready for the challenge.

Although it is not known for sure, it is suggested that it was around this time that Harriet conducted several "passengers" right to the door of the famed abolitionist Frederick Douglass. Like Harriet Tubman, Douglass was also from Maryland. He grew up on a plantation where he was forced to toil in slavery until, one day, he made a break for it by stowing away on a train car.

It is a bit ironic that a man who would become involved in the Underground Railroad first found his freedom on the actual railroad, but this is what happened. It was after disembarking from that train car in New York that Douglass came into contact with an early "conductor" of the Underground Railroad by the name of David Ruggles. Mr. Ruggles was one of the founders of an organization dedicated to the complete eradication of slavery, known as the New York Committee of Vigilance.

According to Frederick Douglass, he "had been in New York but a few days" before David Ruggles befriended him and gave him a place to stay at a boarding house that he operated. So it was that Fredrick Douglass would come to pay it forward and help runaway slaves just as he himself had been helped.

Mr. Douglass lived in Rochester, New York, at the time, which would put him on the path that Harriet may have taken to Canada. And he himself seems to verify this event later by describing a group that seemed to match that of Harriet's.

He later recalled, "On one occasion I had eleven fugitives at the same time under my roof, and it was necessary for them to remain with me until I could collect sufficient money to get them on to Canada. It was the largest number I ever had at any one time, and I had some difficulty in providing so many with food and shelter."

It is believed that after a brief stay with Frederick Douglass, Harriet and those under her charge headed for the Canadian border. They then crossed through Niagara Falls before arriving in St. Catharines, Ontario, in December of 1851. Here they met up with an important contact from the Underground Railroad, a certain Reverend Hiram Wilson. Hiram Wilson was an active agent for the American Anti-Slavery Society, and he had extensive abolitionist contacts in Canada.

It was in light of the Fugitive Slave Act, which had rendered runaways in the North to be even more vulnerable, that Hiram Wilson decided to set up a base in St. Catharines to help those who planned to venture across the border for freedom. Wilson would be pivotal in helping Tubman and those she brought with her to find appropriate lodging and work. Tubman herself probably worked as a cook or housekeeper, or perhaps in another similar post that she had held in the past.

As successful as this foray up the Underground Railroad had been, it is believed that it could have very well ended in disaster. Tubman's later biographer, Sarah Bradford, stated that it was on a trip just like this one that Harriet and the passengers she conducted were almost captured. According to Bradford, on a rescue mission that had Harriet in the company of "several stout men," Tubman suddenly had a premonition of imminent danger.

Instead of traveling on her route like she normally would have, Tubman suddenly announced that God had told her to "stop." Heeding the voice that she heard, she did just that. She then asked that inner voice what she should do. The answer? Harriet claimed that God told her to "leave the road, and turn to the left."

Without question, she obeyed, and she had those following her make an abrupt left turn. A few moments later, she had to stop again because their path was blocked by a stream of water. Since there was no bridge or boat to aid them across, she asked God once again, "What should I do?" According to Harriet, God told her to wade through the water.

The water was most certainly cold during the winter of 1851/52, and it's said that it came all the way up to her shoulders when she waded into it. Those that saw her in the water refused to follow at this point until they saw her—their Moses—cross the river first. They all stood "safe on the opposite shore" and waited until Harriet crossed.

Seeing that it was safe, as they had no wish to get swept away by the current, the group then followed her lead. According to Bradford, they soon came across a second stream.

Some have since claimed that the old spiritual hymn "Wade in the Water" was directly inspired by this event. It certainly isn't hard to imagine Harriet and her charges crossing the river when listening to the lyrics. "Wade in the water...Wade in the water children...Wade in the water."

At any rate, once they safely traversed this stream, Bradford tells us that Harriet "came upon a cabin of colored people, who took them all in, put them to bed, and dried their clothes." It's said that Harriet had nothing to give these kind strangers to show her gratitude save her undergarments. According to Bradford, she gave them some of her "underclothes" that had been hung out to dry as a token of her gratitude.

Sarah Bradford relates that it was later discovered that Harriet's pursuers were hot on her trail, and if she hadn't deviated from her planned course and just "happened upon" the kind family that gave them shelter, she and her whole group could have very well been captured. Bradford and others have insinuated that this was a form of clairvoyance, or spiritual intuitiveness, on Harriet's part. Or, as Bradford put it, "To say the least, there was something remarkable in these facts, whether clairvoyance, or the divine impression on her mind from the source of all power, I cannot tell."

Whatever the case may be, these special directives that Harriet received proved crucial during her many marches toward freedom. During Harriet's multiple long journeys up and down the Underground Railroad, she faced treacherous terrain, search dogs, and bands of roving slave hunters on her trail, brandishing shotguns. The fact that she could brag that she "never lost a passenger" during all her forays up and down the Railroad indicates that there was something very special about Harriet Tubman.

In later years, some of her contemporaries attested to the fact that she just might have even predicted the Emancipation Proclamation that ended slavery, as her vision happened three years before the proclamation was actually issued. According to legend, Tubman was in the company of abolitionist Reverend Henry Highland Garnet when she reported to him a powerful vision of all of the slaves being freed. Harriet Tubman suddenly came down the stairs that morning, filling the whole house with the most joyful of songs, as she sang out loud, "My people are free! My people are free!" She then sat down at the table for breakfast, repeatedly singing those words. Garnet, who took a much more pessimistic outlook on the matter, actually chastised her, saying, "Oh, Harriet! Harriet! You've come to torment us before the time; do cease this noise! My grandchildren may see the day of the emancipation of our people, but you and I will never see it." However, Harriet steadfastly insisted, "I tell you, sir, you'll see it, and you'll see it soon."

Many today might not realize just how grim of an outlook most abolitionists had back then when it came to how long it would take to finally end slavery. Even at the outbreak of the Civil War, many believed that once it was all said and done, the North and South would go right back to the status quo. No one really expected President Abraham Lincoln to declare his Emancipation Proclamation. Yet Harriet seemingly envisioned all of this transpiring well before it actually happened.

After becoming an established fixture in Canada, one of Tubman's biggest expeditions was in 1854 when Harriet Tubman helped her siblings, Ben, Robert, and Henry, to freedom. She showed up at the Maryland plantation on Christmas Eve and located her brothers at her dad's residence. She also managed to convince three additional slaves to tag along as well.

Harriet's dad, meanwhile, had been sworn to silence, and it was repeatedly imparted on him to not tell Harriet's mother about it since she would no doubt worry and perhaps even try to get her children to come back. Her mother had actually been painstakingly preparing a Christmas meal for her sons in the hopes that they would come and see her over the holiday. But as Harriet would later recall, her mother, unfortunately, spent a sad holiday alone.

According to Tubman, "She was looking for 'em all day, an' her heart was mos' broke about 'em." Benjamin Ross, on the other hand, knowing full well where his sons were, proved that he was fully capable of keeping a secret, and when he was asked about his sons' whereabouts, he was quick to tell his taskmasters that, "He hadn't seen one of 'em dis Christmas." Some accounts say that Benjamin, who was a deeply religious man, would never willingly lie, so in order to keep from doing so, he kept his eyes blindfolded while he was around Harriet and her brothers prior to their departure. It was by way of doing this that he could honestly say to all who may be concerned that he "hadn't seen one of 'em dis Christmas."

Harriet and her latest group of freedom seekers arrived in Philadelphia, Pennsylvania, a few days later. From there, they were brought to Harriet's home in St. Catharines, Canada. Upon their arrival, her three siblings took on the last name of Stewart as a means of concealing their identity.

According to later biographers, as much as Harriet's brothers were glad for their newfound freedom, they were off to a rough start. It was extremely cold, and her siblings' only means of making money was to chop wood in the freezing forests of Canada. Harriet did her best to aid them, however, making money in whatever odd jobs she took, which helped to sustain them well enough to make it through the rough winter.

It was around the fall of 1856 that Tubman is said to have helped conduct a former slave by the name of Tilly to the North. According to later recollection, it was said that Harriet was on one of her "stopovers" on the Railroad in New York when she was approached by a former slave who requested her to help bring his fiancé Tilly to freedom.

The man then related how a few years prior, he himself escaped the plantation where he had met Tilly, as his former owner was trying to sell him downriver to the Deep South. These themes of family separation brought on by cruel and uncaring slave owners were certainly something that Harriet was familiar with and could relate to. As such, she didn't hesitate to lend a helping hand.

Using her contacts from the Railroad, she managed to get Tilly on a boat and sail her straight to Delaware, where Tilly would be safely escorted to freedom in Philadelphia. It wasn't all smooth sailing (no pun intended), however, since, during a stopover at Baltimore's Inner Harbor, they had to face the scrutiny of men who may very well have been slave catchers. Their only defense was a set of fabricated "free papers" that Tubman carried with her, stating that they were "free residents."

At one point, it seemed like the captain was going to see through their deception, having them "stand aside and wait for the other passengers to board." It seemed as if the captain was going to call in the slave catchers to have them arrested at any moment. It was during this nerve-racking interlude that Tubman cried out to God. She later reflected that she prayed quite earnestly, "Oh Lord, you been with me in six troubles, don't desert me in the seventh."

In this prayer, Tubman was actually recalling the "six calamities" faced by the biblical figure of Job from the Bible. Even though Harriet couldn't read, she was very aware of the biblical accounts, which she had long ago memorized from the preachings she had heard as a child. So it was that she was once again drawing on her faith, and even while poor Tilly is said to have gone into a full-blown panic attack, Harriet Tubman remained firm as she prayed for their deliverance.

And it seemed to work. Because the next thing they knew, a completely pleasant and respectful captain asked them to step aboard the ship for their departure. Thanks to Harriet, Tilly was soundly delivered to her freedom.

Harriet's dad Benjamin, meanwhile, managed to finally purchase the freedom of Harriet's mother for twenty dollars. The idea that human life was valued so low is nothing short of appalling, but this was the sad state of affairs of the American South at the time. Despite the couple's newfound freedom, Harriet's parents initially remained right where they were.

However, Benjamin Ross served as a vital resource right where he was, as he helped to aid others as they made their way north. In fact, Benjamin proved to be very instrumental in a rescue Harriet made in November of 1856. Ross had made the acquaintance of a slave by the name of Joe Bailey. Joe had just been bought by a new owner, a wealthy farmer by the name of William R. Hughlett, who was particularly cruel and hot-tempered. Joe mentioned to Benjamin his desire for both him and his brother, who was also named William and who was owned by a different slave owner, to escape.

Benjamin then alerted Harriet, and on November 15th, she met up with the brothers and safely conducted them to the North. Joe Bailey's owner, meanwhile, was infuriated since he had just shelled out some two thousand dollars to buy Joe, and now that he had run away, his investment was lost. Seeking to recoup his losses, he posted a reward for $1,500 for Joe's capture.

Harriet led the brothers to Wilmington, Delaware, and by the time they arrived, the reward signs were already in place to greet them. Realizing that it was too dangerous to have the brothers out in the open, Harriet decided to have them lay low until the coast was clear. In the meantime, she contacted the local abolitionist and patron of the Underground Railroad, Thomas Garrett, requesting his help. It was Garrett who came up with the perfect plan for deliverance.

He had a "carriage filled with bricks and workers" arrive on the scene to pick up Harriet and the two runaways. These supposed "workers" were actually in on the plot and were sent to provide transport, as well as a form of cover. Harriet and the two runaways were able to hide in the midst of a bunch of bricks and hay in the back of the carriage, with no one the wiser. It was in this fashion that the group was driven right over the Niagara Falls Suspension Bridge and into Canada.

As successful as this mission was, however, Harriet's father's luck would soon run out. In March of 1857, Benjamin let nine runaways stay at his residence before they embarked upon the Underground Railroad. It was these very efforts that would come back to haunt him when one of those very same runaways had second thoughts, went back to the plantation, and ratted out Benjamin.

The authorities were just getting ready to have Benjamin Ross arrested when Harriet launched what amounted to a rescue mission to retrieve both her father and her mother. Her parents were at an advanced age at this point, so she could have hardly expected them to walk the long distance. As such, she put together a makeshift horse-drawn carriage that was "fitted out in a primitive style with a straw collar, a pair of old chaise wheels, with a board on the axle to sit on, another board swung with ropes, fastened to the axle, to rest their feet on."

Before reaching Canada, they stopped in Wilmington, Delaware, at the home of the aforementioned abolitionist Thomas Garrett. It was Garrett who sheltered the group over the next few days, giving them a place to rest and food to eat. He also gave them some cash to help ease the burden of their journey. Although Tubman's parents were no doubt glad to be free from the tyranny of the South, it is said that the winter of 1857/58 was particularly hard on Tubman's mother, who "made no secret of her misery."

In light of this distress, Tubman sought out a new property for her family. She found it in nearby Auburn, New York. There she bought a house from none other than US Senator William H. Seward for $1,200. Seward himself was a staunch abolitionist, and he was always striving to do whatever he could to further the cause of ending slavery. His selling terms to Harriet Tubman was generally believed to have been quite favorable back then, but Harriet still had some trouble coming up with the "quarterly payments" that would make her the undisputed owner.

In the meantime, by the end of the 1850s, some of Maryland's slave owners were finally beginning to catch on to what was happening to their slaves. They heard rumors of a "black Moses" who was conducting rescue missions in the middle of the night. They still didn't know that it was Harriet Tubman conducting these forays into their backyard, but they were becoming ever more alert that something was afoot.

It was around this time that Harriet became acquainted with a radical abolitionist by the name of John Brown. Mr. Brown was indeed radical when compared to his peers in the abolitionist movement, as he openly championed the use of violence in ending slavery. Although many biographers skip over this fact, John Brown was involved in the 1855 Pottawatomie Massacre, which was a raid launched on a proslavery outpost along the Pottawatomie Creek in Kansas that left several people dead.

It is believed that Tubman first met Brown sometime in 1858, even though Tubman herself would later claim that she had actually seen Brown beforehand in a "prophetic vision." Harriet claimed she had a strange dream of a snake that suddenly "turned into the head of an old man with a long white beard." According to Harriet, the old man looked at her, "wishful like, just as if he was going to speak to me." She then saw "two other heads" appear that were "smaller and younger." Harriet also dreamed that a "crowd of men" laid siege to the heads, "striking down" the first two before taking out the old man.

Brown would later become infamous for launching the raid Harpers Ferry in October 1859. In this scheme, Brown planned to spark a nationwide slave revolt by seizing a United States arsenal located in Harpers Ferry, Virginia. However, all he managed to do was bring down the wrath of the federal government upon him and others. Brown himself was later executed. Harriet would, admittedly after the fact, claim that the dream she had was prophetic of Brown's fate since his two sons (the little heads) were killed in the raid, and he himself (the old man) was executed later.

Just prior to the Harpers Ferry fiasco, John Brown had accompanied Tubman to meet with an antislavery advocate by the name of Wendell Phillips. Mr. Phillips was an attorney who gave up his formal practice in favor of working full time for the eradication of slavery. Phillips himself was a great leader of the abolitionist cause at the time and quite famous for the stirring speeches that he would give for the furtherance of the antislavery mission.

All the same, Phillips would later recall the incredible intensity with which John Brown introduced Harriet Tubman to him. According to Phillips, Brown presented her by telling him, "Mr. Phillips, I bring you one of the best and bravest persons on this continent—General Tubman, we call her." She was indeed a one-woman army, and soon enough—at least as it pertained to the Underground Railroad—she would show just how pivotal her leadership could be.

Chapter 6 – Harriet on the Front Lines

One of Harriet Tubman's most daring "raids" occurred in the spring of 1860 in Troy, New York, when she helped to free fugitive slave Charles Nalle from captivity. Nalle had been arrested while on the run in New York, and his master had arrived to pick him up. The really bizarre thing about this case was the fact that Charles Nalle's owner was his own brother, Blucher Hansbrough.

It is believed that Blucher's father, Peter, was the one that impregnated Nalle's enslaved mother, while Blucher himself was conceived with Peter's wife. This would have made Blucher Hansbrough the half-brother of Charles Nalle. At any rate, it is said that the two bore a "striking resemblance to each other." Even just a casual glance would tell one that they were related.

And yet, through the horrors of slavery, Charles Nalle was considered property by his own family member. As bad as slavery was, Charles was given a slightly easier life than many others in his condition. He worked with relative ease as a coachman, driving horse-drawn carriages, and he was allowed to travel with his half-brother Blucher far and wide.

But Charles Nalle's real difficulty came when the slave he was married to, a woman named Catherine Simms, was freed. Simms's former owner had left instructions that Catherine and the children she had with Charles Nalle should be freed upon his passing. The only trouble was, according to the laws in Virginia, once a slave was freed, they had to move out of the state within a year. This was devastating for Charles since it meant his whole family would have to move away from him.

His wife and children ended up moving to Washington, DC. Shortly thereafter, his owner, who must have felt at least some form of sympathy for Nalle, gave Charles, as well as another enslaved man named Jim Banks, a one-week pass to go visit Catherine in Washington. But rather than going to DC, Charles and Jim made a break for it and went to New York instead, becoming fugitive slaves in the process.

It turns out that Charles had been helped by someone named Minot S. Crosby, who was a contact for the Underground Railroad. With his help, Charles got a job as a coachman, and he eventually became self-sufficient and began making plans to reunite with his wife and kids. But all of these plans came under siege when an attorney by the name of Horatio Averill was tipped off to what Charles Nalle was doing and notified Blucher about it.

This led Blucher to send a slave catcher after Charles. Charles was then subsequently captured and detained. But little did anyone know that the Underground Railroad had been tipped off as to what was happening, and a crowd—led by none other than Harriet Tubman—began to assemble outside of the Commissioner's Office where Charles was being held. Harriet actually snuck into the building and stood by a window; the crowd was instructed to watch her for cues as to what to do next.

As Harriet Tubman's biographer Sarah Bradford tells it, Harriet disguised herself as an elderly woman, taking on a stooped posture, walking slowly, and covering her face in a bonnet, so that those in the building wouldn't expect anything from her. Even though no one would have suspected it, she was like a fly on the wall and kept up with every single development.

It had been decided meanwhile that Charles needed to be transferred to another building to appear before a judge. It was at this point, right when Charles Nalle was getting ready to exit the building, that Harriet gave the signal. Right when they were exiting, Harriet screamed from the window for all of those assembled down below to hear, "Here they come!" The crowd then converged to block the group from leaving. Tubman herself raced outside and grabbed hold of Charles.

As she held on tight, Tubman then directed the crowd. "Drag us out! Drag him to the river!" In the chaos, the crowd managed to free Charles from his captors and pull him toward the Hudson River. From there, he was put on a boat and taken to the other side. However, those who wished to keep Charles detained had telegraphed people on the other side, alerting them to what had happened. As such, he was recaptured shortly after getting off the boat.

But Harriet and her compatriots weren't about to give up, and after crossing the river themselves, they converged upon the scene and managed to pull Charles free once again. This incredible event was captured in the papers at the time, and it created quite a sensation. At this point, Harriet Tubman had become quite a well-known figure in the abolitionist movement.

And along with her exploits in rescuing slaves, she had also become an accomplished speaker. She regularly shared her experiences with audiences, personalizing and bringing a visible face to the struggle against slavery. One of her more famous speeches from this period occurred in May of 1860 at a conference for the New England Anti-Slavery Society, which was being held in Boston, Massachusetts.

An activist newspaper called *The Liberator* made a note of the event, describing, "A colored woman of the name of Moses, who, herself a fugitive, has eight times returned to the slave states for the purpose of rescuing others from bondage, and who has met with extraordinary success in her efforts, was then introduced. She told the story of her adventures in a modest but quaint and amusing style, which won much applause."

The "Moses" that the paper mentioned was none other than Harriet Tubman. At this point, she had led several exoduses of slaves out of the South, so if anyone should be likened to the slave-freeing biblical patriarch who parted the Red Sea, it should have been Harriet. It was around this time that Harriet Tubman determined to head back to Maryland once again, this time to help bring her little sister Rachel and her two kids to freedom.

Rachel was the very last member of Tubman's family to be on the old Brodess plantation. Due to all of the slaves that had escaped, many of them being related to Tubman, one might think that they would have suspected her. But apparently, no one ever imagined that it was Harriet Tubman who was stealing all of the plantation slaves away in the middle of the night. Some in Maryland even hypothesized that it was some radical white abolitionist who had been absconding with their "property."

But Harriet didn't need their accolades or attention; in fact, she worked best when she was obscure, unknown, and underestimated. She often wore disguises on her journeys and sometimes even made herself appear old and feeble just to escape attention. Whatever it took, she was willing to do it if it meant that she could bring others to freedom, as was the case in 1860 when she set out to retrieve her sister. Sadly enough, however, this objective would not be met.

Upon her arrival, she found that her sister had passed away. She was deeply grieved but still wished to locate her deceased sister's children. But after asking around, she was unable to locate her nieces and nephews. Determined to make something of her efforts, she ended up bringing back a completely different family—Stephen and Maria Ennals and their children.

After this somewhat successful foray came to a close, Harriet spent much of the rest of the year in her Canadian refuge while keeping her eyes and ears peeled to the latest political happenings in America. And in the last few months of 1860, the powder keg of the South was just about ready to blow. It was the US election of a known antislavery sympathizer, Republican Abraham Lincoln, that served as the match to set this conflagration off.

Before Lincoln was even sworn into office, the Southern states began to secede from the Union. First, South Carolina left, soon followed by Mississippi, Florida, Alabama, Georgia, Louisiana, and Texas—all of them seceded, one after the other. This sudden secession set the stage for the Civil War and, in many people's eyes, the final death knell of slavery in the United States. Harriet Tubman, caught up in the fervor of the war, wanted to be a part of it, and she became actively involved with abolitionists in Philadelphia and Boston.

And when the war began in earnest in April of 1861, Tubman was ready to contribute to the Union cause. Her first opportunity to do so came when she received word that the former Confederate stronghold of Port Royal, South Carolina, had been seized by Union troops. This meant that there would be plenty of former slaves seeking their freedom now that their Southern masters had been dispatched.

Realizing that the Union would have a sudden influx of civilian refugees on its hands, Harriet made her way to South Carolina so that she could render her services. The former slaves that she encountered were primarily a group from the Deep South known as the Gullah. This group of African Americans, who still live primarily in the Lowcountry region of Georgia, Florida, and South Carolina, had managed to retain much of their West African culture and dialect.

They spoke a creole language that is said to have contained many African loan words. One of the reasons why this group remained so distinct was the fact that those who worked on the large sprawling plantations in this part of the Deep South were often left isolated and on their own for long periods, which allowed them to retain and reinforce their ancestral culture much easier than slaves in the Upper South.

As interesting as all of this was, Harriet Tubman found that she had a hard time communicating with the Gullah. While Harriet and the Gullah both spoke English, their dialects were so different from each other that it would often create confusion. As she later explained to her biographer Sarah Bradford, "Why, their language down there in the far South is just as different from ours in Maryland as you can think. They laughed when they heard me talk, and I could not understand them, no how."

One of the words unique to the Gullah that initially confounded Harriet was *buckra,* a term the Gullah used to refer to white people. This is actually a word that can be traced directly back to West Africa. But when the Gullah started asking about the "Yankee buckra" that she was with, Harriet at first didn't know what they were talking about. Nevertheless, as she got to know these new arrivals better, she found ways to bridge the divide, and soon, she became well acquainted with them.

During her time in South Carolina, she came under the command of Union General David Hunter. Hunter himself was actually a strident abolitionist who was eager to put an end to slavery once and for all. He was so forward-thinking, in fact, that he advocated for the enlistment of freed African American soldiers before Abraham Lincoln would even consider the notion.

Without waiting for authorization, General Hunter began to actively recruit runaway slaves for a unit of African American troops. This was contrary to Lincoln's wishes at the time, however, since Lincoln had not yet declared the emancipation of slavery in the Southern states. He soon would, of course, but his initial hesitation provoked a rebuke from none other than Harriet Tubman.

> Master Lincoln, he's a great man, and I am a poor negro; but the negro can tell master Lincoln how to save the money and the young men. He can do it by setting the negro free. Suppose that was an awful big snake down there on the floor. He bite you. Folks all scared, because you die. You send for a doctor to cut the bite; but the snake, he rolled up there, and

while the doctor doing it, he bite you again. The doctor dug out that bite; but while the doctor doing it, the snake, he spring up and bite you again; so he keep doing it, till you kill him. That's what master Lincoln ought to know.

In the metaphor Harriet used, the snake was meant to symbolize the South and the institution of slavery. If Lincoln did not get rid of this snake, Tubman asserted that it would just keep springing back up to strike again and again. She wanted Lincoln to know that if he really wanted to beat the South, then he needed to beat and abolish the institution of slavery—there was no other way.

While Lincoln dithered on declaring the ultimate emancipation of slaves, Harriet meanwhile became proactive, putting forth her services as a nurse at Port Royal. Here, she concocted natural remedies just like her own mother did when she was a child, and she used them to treat everything from diarrhea to smallpox outbreaks. Harriet had a great knack for utilizing amazing natural remedies to treat just about any condition.

One source would later recall an instance in which Harriet seemingly healed someone's half-severed thumb by wrapping it up in cobwebs and a piece of cloth. The idea of Harriet running around looking for cobwebs and then wrapping up wounds with them might strike one as a little strange. But, as it turns out, this is a folk remedy that has merit. Cobwebs have a tremendous healing ability. Spider webs are naturally loaded with vitamin K, which is crucial when it comes to stopping the flow of blood from open wounds. It's for this reason that securing spider webs over a wound and applying the pressure of a piece of cloth will naturally help the wound to coagulate and allow the body to speed up the healing process. Spider webs also have the benefit of being made of natural antiseptic material, which helps to reduce any risk of infection when applied to wounds.

This is something that the medical establishment of today has only just recently confirmed. But long before modern science caught on, Harriet, through the lore of her ancestors, as well as through trial and error, intuitively knew that spider webs had this magical healing property. And she was right. Because when she applied it to the person with the half-severed thumb, rather than having to have the digit amputated, her patient had a speedy recovery.

For her services as a nurse, it is said that she only received a total of two hundred dollars. She also received regular rations, but she ended up declining to take them so that they could be given to her "less fortunate neighbors" instead. In truth, she was afraid that some of the former slaves she treated would be resentful of her, perceiving her as receiving special treatment from the white officers.

In order to make a little extra money, she actually began cooking up gingerbread, pies, and homemade root beer, which she would then have another person market to the troops. Ever the entrepreneur, when she didn't have a steady paycheck, she always found a way to raise enough funds when she needed them.

When Lincoln freed the slaves with his Emancipation Proclamation in January of 1863, Harriet was inspired to throw her lot in with the Union Army even more, and she cobbled together a group of spies that she worked with to go into the South and gather intel on the enemy.

Harriet was a face that the slaves of the South could trust, and she managed to blend into their communities quite well. According to her biographer Sarah Bradford, "She gained the confidence of the slaves by her cheery words, and songs, and sacred hymns, and obtained from them much valuable information." Harriet's network was able to provide detailed information on enemy positions, the location of supply depots, and how to navigate through rugged terrain.

Many Union victories can be credited to the ability of the North to tap into this refined resource of human reconnaissance. According to Bradford, Harriet exhibited "faithfulness and bravery, and her untiring zeal for the welfare of our soldiers, black and white." At one point, Harriet was even used as a kind of guide through some of the more remote and inhospitable regions of the South.

The same General Hunter that Harriet had worked with before requested her to help guide a group of gunboats through the

Combahee River. This she did under the supervision of Union Colonel James Montgomery in June of 1863. There is some irony in Harriet's pairing with James Montgomery since the two both had a mutual acquaintance with the late John Brown.

As strange as it may seem, this Union colonel had actually fought alongside John Brown—a man executed by the federal government for treason—during the 1850s in a spate of conflicts known as Bleeding Kansas or the Border War. This was a series of violent battles that erupted in the aftermath of the Kansas-Nebraska Act of 1854, which created the territories of Nebraska and Kansas.

However, that wasn't the only thing the act addressed. In those days, whenever a new territory was incorporated into the United States, the big question that was on everyone's mind was whether or not the new territory would allow slavery. And when Kansas, in particular, became a US territory, the question loomed large as to which direction Kansas would go. Would the territory become a slave or free state? Since the passage of the Kansas-Nebraska Act effectively ended the Missouri Comprise, which prohibited slavery north of the $36°30'$ parallel, this meant the people in these territories would have to make their own decision when it came to the issue of slavery. The Territory of Nebraska was firmly in the orbit of the North, but Kansas was more in line with the South, and many Southerners wanted to make sure it was ideologically in line with the Southern practice of slavery as well.

And as pro-slavery forces began to converge on the territory, many antislavery-leaning settlers began to flock to the area too. Like the convergence of matter and antimatter, this created an incredibly hostile environment, as it was made up of individuals who were radically opposed to each other, and as such, a terrible conflict was just waiting to erupt. And all hell would break loose in March of 1855 when thousands of so-called "Border Ruffians" infiltrated Kansas from the pro-slave state of Missouri and set about creating a pro-slavery legislature.

This gave the control to the pro-slavery forces, and they quickly made it against Kansas law to so much as even speak out against slavery. When the abolitionists tried to protest these conditions in 1856 from their base in Lawrence, Kansas, the Border Ruffians rushed in and violently assaulted them, burning down printing presses and causing overall distress. Future Union Colonel James Montgomery, meanwhile, had bought some land in Kansas and had become involved with an antislavery group known as the Free-Staters who took up arms against the pro-slavery Border Ruffians.

It was in this conflict that Montgomery became acquainted with John Brown, and he developed a lasting respect for the radical abolitionist. In fact, Montgomery admired Brown so much that Colonel Montgomery made sure to mention his association with Brown to Harriet Tubman. He talked about how he and Brown led daring raids on the slaveholders and how they were called Jayhawkers. They were called this because the Jayhawk is a reference to a bird that steals the nest of another bird. He and Brown were labeled as Jayhawks because they plundered goods from slavers and burned down their properties.

For the impending Union raids of Southern plantations, Colonel Montgomery planned to do very much the same. Montgomery's contingent included a large group of African American soldiers, and it was noted for its historic deployment of African American servicemen. But most historic of all was their brave commander Harriet Tubman, who would go down in history as "the first woman to lead an armed military operation." Not only did Harriet know the lay of the land, but she also had operatives that could inform her of where the explosive mines set by the Confederates would be.

This proved to be invaluable to the North as they made their way across the Combahee River. This expedition not only removed these obstacles, but it also struck a blow to the South by allowing Union troops to raid rebel supply depots, depriving the enemy of their own goods. As a correspondent working for the *Wisconsin State Journal* later described the whole episode. "Colonel Montgomery and his gallant band of 300 black soldiers, under the guidance of a black woman, dashed into the enemies' country, struck a bold and effective blow, destroying millions of dollars' worth of commissary stores, cotton, and lordly dwellings, and striking terror to the heart of the rebellion, brought off nearly 800 slaves and thousands of dollars' worth of property, without losing a man or receiving a scratch!"

The way the article described the situation makes it seem as if the Union coerced the former slaves to come with them. But, in reality, once those in bondage realized that these Union ships could bring them to freedom, no coercion was needed. As soon as the slaves in the area received word that the gunboats were from Lincoln, they started crowding around, seeking their deliverance.

Harriet described the chaotic scene herself.

> I never seen such a sight. We laughed, an' laughed, an' laughed [Harriet and her companions in the gunboat]. Here you'd see a woman with a pail on her head, rice a' smoking in it, just as [if] she'd taken it from the fire, young one hanging on behind, one hangin' round her forehead to hold on, another hand diggin' into the rice-pot eating with all it's might; hold of her dress two or three more; down her back a bag with a pig in it. One woman brought two pigs, a white one and a black one; we took them all on board; named the white pig Beauregard, and the black pig Jeff Davis.

The latter reference was, of course, to Confederate President Jefferson Davis.

At one point, in the midst of all this, the refugees got to be a little too much for the Union troops to handle, and Montgomery allegedly ordered Harriet Tubman to "sing to them" in order to "calm them down." As odd as it may seem, Harriet supposedly ad-libbed the following words on the spot, singing, "Of all the whole creation in the East or in the West...The Glorious Yankee nation is the greatest and the best...Come along! Come along! Don't be alarmed! Uncle Sam is rich enough to give you all a farm!"

One has to wonder if that last refrain was in reference to the unfilled promise of the North to give all of the former slaves their own self-sustaining farms—the often-quoted "40 acres and a mule." Sadly, no matter how much Harriet Tubman may have sung about such things, these plans would never be fulfilled. In reality, the freed slaves were freed with little more than the clothes on their back and whatever they could carry in their weary arms.

Having said that, as much as Tubman later laughed at the freed slaves carrying pots of rice and a "pig in a bag" slung over their backs, they had good reason to bring these rations and supplies with them. Those who loaded up on such goods were later on much thankful for the effort, as they would be penniless upon their liberation.

Along with these daring adventures, Harriet also routinely engaged in more mundane work, which was still just as vital, helping to wash clothes and cook food for the troops. It was Tubman, in fact, that cooked up the last meal of the famed colonel of the all-black 54th Regiment of Massachusetts, Robert Gould Shaw. This was a scene that was immortalized in the 1989 Civil War movie *Glory.*

It was after eating this meal served up by Tubman that Colonel Gould and his men charged into what would be a climactic battle, known as the Second Battle of Fort Wagner, that resulted in the deaths of 1,500 Union men, some of which were African American. Harriet would later give her own account of the fighting in some rather stark terms. "Then we saw the lightning, and that was the guns; and then we heard the thunder, and that was the big guns; and then we heard the rain falling, and that was the drops of blood falling; and when we came to get in the crops, it was dead men that we reaped."

Harriet herself was no doubt growing weary of all of the carnage, and by the spring of 1864, she requested a leave of absence so that she could return to her home in Auburn, New York. It was around this time that most believe that Sarah Bradford first conducted interviews with Tubman, which would ultimately become the 1869 biography, *Scenes in the Life of Harriet Tubman.*

Bradford was actually a teacher at a local school in Auburn at the time. When she became acquainted with Harriet Tubman, she was immediately stirred and inspired by her story. She was also aware that Tubman could use the proceeds the book sales might bring her, so she didn't hesitate to put Tubman's life's work into the printed format of a book. It is said that the proceeds from this book brought in around one thousand dollars to aid Harriet's financial needs at the time.

It seems that Sarah Bradford's intentions were good when it came to writing Harriet's biography, but many today would be offended by some of the language and attitudes that she presented while compiling Harriet's life story. Most glaring is the fact that Bradford continually insists that Harriet was a rare commodity "among her people." Bradford also declared the following statement, which is particularly insulting today.

> I am quite willing to acknowledge that she was almost an anomaly among her people, but I have known many of her family, and so far as I can judge they all seem to be peculiarly intelligent, upright and religious people, and to have a strong feeling of family affection. There may be many among the colored race like them; certainly, all should not be judged by the idle, miserable darkies who have swarmed about Washington and other cities since the War.

Anyone reading such a passage like this in the modern day would be offended on multiple levels. Bradford was basically using the prejudiced "she's a credit to her race" sentiment that became common during her time period. Those with such views tended to view great African American leaders as the exception and not the rule. By saying such things, Bradford, who was a friend of Tubman's no less, was expressing that same ugly sentiment.

And, of course, her mention of "miserable darkies" overrunning Washington, DC, in the aftermath of the Civil War is obviously offensive in the extreme. After the end of the Civil War, there was indeed a massive influx of refugees that "swarmed" the nation's capital because these recently freed slaves literally had nowhere else to go. Bradford shows both a lack of compassion and a lack of understanding in suggesting that these poor souls were merely "idle" as they sought refuge in the one place they thought would be safe.

In reality, these vulnerable refugees were doing the best they could, considering the conditions and circumstances they came from. They had just been freed from a life of slavery, but they didn't have any money or any education—most of them couldn't read or write—and it was an uphill struggle for them to find a decent paying job that could support themselves, let alone their family. Harriet Tubman understood that these difficulties would arise even before the war ended.

Unlike many of the Northern post-war planners, who didn't take into consideration what might befall former slaves once they were free, Harriet understood very well that the recently freed slaves needed to be given some means to earn an income once they were freed. This is why she spent much of her time in the last couple years of the war training recently freed slaves in tasks that they could later use as a profitable vocation.

Perhaps the greatest tragedy of all is that those war-torn refugees that Bradford calls "idle" wouldn't have been so listless if the federal government had simply made good on their original promise of granting every single freed slave forty acres and a mule. At any rate, if Harriet Tubman had been able to read what this woman actually wrote, there's a good chance she would have objected to the tone and direction that Bradford took with her life narrative.

After sitting down for these interviews with Bradford in the summer of 1864, Harriet made a trip to Boston, Massachusetts, where she made the acquaintance of another famous African American activist, Sojourner Truth. Sojourner Truth had become quite well known on the lecture circuit, where she voiced her views on everything from abolition, to women's equality, to religious matters.

Interestingly enough, shortly after this meeting, both Sojourner and Harriet were invited to meet with President Abraham Lincoln.

Sojourner went, but Harriet refused. Many today might be surprised to hear this, but Harriet actually believed that Lincoln hadn't done enough "to free the slaves." Despite the general view of Abraham Lincoln today as the "great emancipator," his decision to free enslaved Americans actually took some time to evolve.

When the war first began, Lincoln actually denied that he intended to disrupt the institution of slavery. He initially claimed that he just wanted to bring the seceding states back to the Union. It wasn't until 1863 that Lincoln finally came around to the idea that slavery must be forcibly ended once and for all. As such, African American leaders like Harriet were inclined to feel that Lincoln was too slow to act.

Harriet's contemporary Sojourner Truth, on the other hand, begged to differ. Sojourner Truth gave Lincoln much more leeway on the issue of emancipation and didn't hold it against the president for his delay in formalizing the motion. Sojourner Truth, in fact, went on the campaign trail for Abraham Lincoln in 1864, helping to ensure that the wartime president would be reelected.

As the war was drawing to a close, the biggest subject on the mind of many, including Harriet Tubman, was just what would happen to all of the slaves that had just been freed. They may have been led to freedom, but most had no idea of how to support themselves in the aftermath. They needed to learn some kind of trade so they would be able to get paying jobs that they needed to support themselves.

Some wanted to be lenient on the Southern powers that be and not push them very hard when it came to honoring the civil rights of African Americans, while others sought a more comprehensive program to aid the newly freed slaves. Some of the most vocal proponents of the latter camp were the Radical Republicans. It was Abraham Lincoln's Republican Party that waged the war against the slaveholding South and championed the idea of abolishing slavery in the first place.

The South, by contrast, was dominated by Democrats, who sought to curtail the rights of the recently-freed African Americans at every turn. Many today might be surprised by this since the modern

Democratic Party is rightfully associated with supporting the civil rights movement under John F. Kennedy and Lyndon B. Johnson in the 1960s. But suffice it to say, the Democratic Party of the 1960s was a whole lot different than the one of the 1860s.

To put it simply, during the 1860s, the Democratic Party was the party of the former slaveholders, and the Republicans were the champions of civil rights and the empowerment of African Americans. And none were more outspoken about these rights than the Radical Republicans, who were led by a senator from Massachusetts by the name of Charles Sumner.

As the concept of Reconstruction was still being formulated, Sumner unequivocally stated the following:

> It is evident, then that the freedmen are not idlers. They desire work. But in their helpless condition they have not the ability to obtain it without assistance. They are alone, friendless, and uninformed. The curse of slavery is still upon them. Somebody must take them by the hand; not to support them but simply to help them to that work which will support them. Without such intervention, many of those poor people, freed by our acts in the exercise of a military necessity, will be let to perish.

If Harriet was a US representative at the time, she would have, without a doubt, been a Radical Republican, voicing the same opinion as Sumner, and she would have pushed the Lincoln administration to do more to help rehabilitate former slaves. Nevertheless, despite her political differences with Lincoln, Harriet Tubman still did everything she could to help expedite the freedom of her people, and after her brief rest, she quickly went back to work on the front lines, tending the sick and gathering valuable intelligence for the war effort.

Toward the very end of the war, in the summer of 1865, she was instructed to go to James River Hospital in Virginia, where she once again served as a nurse for a fresh influx of veterans. The veterans she treated greatly admired her, and all of them held her in high regard for her selfless service. Although she was never paid for her efforts, she still would render aid to all who needed it. No matter what challenge she may have been presented with, Harriet Tubman was more than ready to march right off to the front lines and face it, head-on.

Chapter 7 – With the Help of Her Family and Friends

The Civil War ended on April 9th, 1865, when beleaguered Confederate General Robert E. Lee signed his name off on an official declaration of surrender at the Appomattox Courthouse in Virginia. Harriet Tubman, like many others, was elated at the news. But soon, this joy would turn to sorrow, as a few days later, on April 14th, 1865, President Abraham Lincoln was killed by an assassin's bullet. Although Harriet Tubman was critical of Lincoln's handling of the emancipation of slaves, she, too, would come to grieve this loss.

She was serving at a hospital at the time, and she would later recall the reaction of those around her—most especially the recently freed African Americans. In one incident, she would relate how she saw an old African American man immediately fall down on the ground upon hearing the news, crying out to God, "We kneel upon the ground, with our faces in our hands, and our hands in the dust, and cry to thee for mercy, O' Lord, this evening."

Harriet herself would suffer violence a short time later, but it was not from a former Confederate or Southern sympathizer. Rather, the conflict was committed by a few prejudiced Northerners in New York. Harriet was taking a train from Auburn to New York City when a couple of passengers and the train's conductor forcibly expelled her from the train.

It remains a little unclear as to how exactly the dispute arose, but Tubman had what sources refer to as a "valid half-price ticket," but once she took a seat on the train, the conductor came back and started giving her a hard time. He apparently ordered her to get up and sit in the smoking car—sometimes referred to as a baggage car, where African Americans were usually forced to sit—instead.

Harriet Tubman, a woman who had just served on the front lines in the Civil War, was now being treated like a second-class citizen. One can only imagine how upsetting this must have been for her. And when she tried to stand up for herself, the conductor proceeded to use racial slurs and spoke to her in the vilest of terms. Despite the abuse, Tubman still refused to move, and that's when the conductor got violent, and with the help of two passengers, they began to manhandle her, yanking her from her seat.

While Harriet screamed and cried out, they threw her into the baggage car. Some passengers were so cruel that they even joked about throwing her off the train. The idea that these passengers could be so callous as to even jest about throwing this unoffending woman off the train is sickening, to say the least. Besides the psychological trauma she endured, Harriet suffered a broken arm and sustained damage to her ribcage from the altercation.

Injured and stuck in New York, she was forced to stay where she was until she had healed enough to try to head for Auburn once again. Her friends and family were naturally enraged by the abuse she suffered, and one of them even looked into getting an attorney so that they could sue the railroad.

But these plans fell through when it became clear that none of the potential witnesses to the incident were going to cooperate. This was, of course, long before the days of security cameras in public transit, so without anyone vouching for what had happened to her, Harriet had no way to prove her case. The assault she suffered continued to affect her both physically and psychologically, which, in turn, affected her financially since she found herself unable to work.

Fearing that she would lose her house in Auburn, she often had to rely on whatever donations her supporters gave her. At one point, Harriet was so discouraged that she "shut herself up in her closest" and prayed to God for some kind of deliverance. Her faith in God had always come through for her before, so why wouldn't it now?

Confident that God would provide, Harriet got out of her closet and informed her hungry lodgers, "We're going to have soup today." Harriet then picked up an empty basket and headed for the local marketplace. She had no money, but trusting in God, she browsed through the produce as if she did. At one point, a butcher gave her a soup bone, telling her to simply "pay him when she could."

After this, it was like a chain reaction was set off, and several other sellers did the same thing. The next thing she knew, her basket was loaded up with more than enough ingredients for the preparation of a good hearty batch of soup. Was it divine intervention that allowed Harriet and her household to have soup that day? She, no doubt, believed it was. But Harriet was not one to push her luck, even when it came to divinity.

She knew that God liked to help those who also helped themselves. And so, in order to better remedy her situation, Harriet began to press the federal government to pay her for her service during the war. Since she was not designated as an official member of the military, she was not paid a pension as other veterans would be. However, considering the role that she played, she deserved some form of payment, as she was just as active during the war than any other soldier had been.

Aiding Harriet in her cause were several of her abolitionist associates, who, while drafting special petitions on her behalf, asked not only for a current pension but also backpay for all of the previous months that she had not been given any money. Meanwhile, as she began to mend, Harriet got back to work as best she could, tending to a large garden outside of her house. She had quite the green thumb when it came to cultivation and was able to make a good amount of money selling her harvest every year.

Another way she managed to raise funds was by renting out spare rooms of her house to guests passing through the region. It was actually through this enterprise that she met her future husband. One of these house guests was a man by the name of Nelson Davis. Mr. Davis was himself a Civil War veteran and ended up leasing his room at Harriet's Auburn home for a span of over three years.

After the war came to a close, Nelson Davis struggled to get on his feet. He tried his luck working as a bricklayer, but he had issues with being able to stay on the job. Besides the difficulties that all veterans of terrible wars face, Nelson was particularly troubled by regular bouts of tuberculosis. As caring of a soul as Harriet was, she no doubt took Nelson under her wing and tried her best to nurse him back to health.

Harriet Tubman's first husband, John Tubman, meanwhile had passed away in 1867. It's said that he was killed in an altercation after he got into an argument with a white Southerner. Sadly, the all-white jury found his killer "not guilty." The story was such a sensation at the time that it was mentioned in the local newspaper, the *Baltimore American*. Unfortunately, John Tubman's death would be just one of many that would befall African American men in the American South as Southerners began to aggressively reassert themselves.

Even though the Confederates had lost the war, and the slaves were now freed, the Southerners would begin to clamp down so hard on the rights of these freedmen and women that they could scarcely tell the difference. Harriet Tubman was, of course, shocked and outraged to hear of what had happened to her former husband. He may have not always treated her the best, but she most certainly never wanted him to go through what he did. But at any rate, with the death of John Tubman, Harriet finally felt the time had come for her to move on.

Although Harriet is said to have been about twenty years Nelson Davis's senior at the time, the two grew to care a great deal for each other. And as their love and commitment for each other grew, they decided to make their relationship official, getting married in the year

1869. Their wedding ceremony was held in the Central Presbyterian Church and was attended by many well-wishers. Shortly after their marriage, Davis started his own brickmaking business, and he busied himself by getting on the board of a local African American church, where he was eventually elected as a trustee.

Nelson and Harriet never had any biological children, but in 1874, they adopted a baby girl by the name of Gertie. It should be noted that Harriet Tubman is not known to have had any biological children on her own, but her and Nelson's love of their adopted child more than made up for that fact.

Gertie herself presents a bit of an enigma for historians. No one knows for sure how Harriet came across the girl or if she was even legally adopted. All we know is that Harriet considered the baby girl to be "adopted" in 1874. Not much else is said of the child, however. All we have is an old photograph from 1888 that shows Gertie at around fourteen years of age, standing by Harriet and a seated—and already sickly-looking—Nelson Davis. The only other mention of her in the historical record is that she became married in 1900, with her name changing from Gertie Davis to Gertie Watson.

It doesn't appear that Gertie and Harriet were all that close in her later years, as there is no mention of her. Strangely, it seems that her adopted child all but disappeared from her life. But some would say that the mystery of Gertie pales in comparison when it comes to Harriet's mysterious so-called niece Margaret. Harriet allegedly rescued Margaret on one of her expeditions back to Maryland in 1859, but Margaret's daughter Alice would later claim that her mother was essentially kidnapped from her parents. As you can see, much of Harriet's personal life still remains unknown, and it provides a topic of endless debate among historians.

At any rate, just as Harriet was establishing her own personal family, her parents passed away, with her father Benjamin Ross dying in 1871, and her mother and namesake Harriet passing in 1879. Both lived long lives, well into their nineties, and they were made as comfortable in their senior years as possible, all thanks to the efforts of their dedicated and dutiful daughter, Harriet Tubman.

But having said that, Tubman had a lot on her shoulders, and by the time she herself began to feel the weight of age, she often found herself struggling financially. It was largely due to her financial difficulty that she found herself susceptible to two smooth-talking conmen who lured her into a get-rich-quick scheme. Known as Mr. Stevenson and John Thomas, these guys made up a story about having gold that they recovered in South Carolina from the Confederates.

They said that the gold was worth five thousand dollars, but they were willing to sell it to Harriet for just two thousand dollars. Most would probably see some pretty crimson red flags right then and there. Why in the world, after all, would someone something worth five thousand dollars for two thousand dollars? According to the scammers, the reason was due to the fact that federal agents would seize the gold from them if they found out about it, so it was for this reason that they wanted to quickly exchange the contraband for a discounted amount.

At any rate, Harriet, desperate for cash, was apparently conned into believing their story. For her, the story had a ring of truth to it. She knew from personal experience that rich Southerners were known to have hidden their treasure right before the Union Army came in. She also knew that African Americans like Stevenson and Thomas were regularly posted on sites like this to dig and search for contraband.

So, in Harriet's mind, their account seemed at least somewhat feasible. Thus, believing that she could be on the verge of a deal of a lifetime, she borrowed two thousand dollars from a rich associate of hers by the name of Anthony Shimer and set up a date to meet the two gentlemen to buy their gold.

Anthony Shimer, Nelson Davis, one of Harriet's brothers, and another friend of theirs all accompanied Harriet to bear witness to this transaction. She didn't know the man that well, of course, so this would seem reasonable enough. But unfortunately, somewhere along the way, the dastardly duo of Stevenson and Thomas tricked Harriet into meeting with them "deep in the woods." They told her this was where they had hidden the treasure, and they didn't want anyone else to see it. Surely, her husband Nelson must have been concerned to allow his wife to go by herself on such a venture, but one can only imagine headstrong Harriet assuring him that she would be fine. She had survived the rigors of the Underground Railroad after all. What could these two strange men possibly do to her?

Unfortunately, she made a grave misjudgment of the situation. As soon as she got into the deep woods with these men, she realized her mistake. There was no gold. The men opened up the trunk they carried, revealing nothing but a box full of rocks. The men then grabbed hold of her and used chloroform to knock her unconscious before taking her purse and tying her up.

Just like the crooks that ambush folks on Craigslist today, these con artists gained Harriet's trust in what she thought was an honest venture, only to be seriously taken advantage of. Her husband, brother, and friends found her a short time later, battered, bruised, tied up, and gagged in the middle of the forest. It must have been a shocking scene for all involved. She thankfully made a full recovery after this assault, but she was out two thousand dollars for her trouble.

Matters would get even worse in 1880 when Harriet and Nelson's home burned down. The cause of the fire is not exactly clear. Some sources say that the blaze may have initiated from a "defective stovepipe that had been struck through a hole in a lintern, to serve as a chimney." But whatever the case may be, it seems to have been completely accidental in nature.

Thankfully, her friends—like they so often did—came to Harriet's aid in her time of need and raised money to help Tubman and her husband rebuild. Nelson was instrumental in this since he personally helped to make the bricks. In many ways, Harriet still lived a hardscrabble life, but as long as she had the support of her friends and family, she never wanted for anything at all.

Chapter 8 – Preparing a Place for Harriet Tubman

After several happy years together, tragedy would strike Harriet in 1888 when her beloved husband Nelson passed away. Nelson was only 44 years old when he passed. Although he had been sick with tuberculosis for quite some time, his final passing came as a shock to all who knew him.

Harriet, of course, deeply grieved this loss, but ironically enough, it was after his death that she would finally receive a pension. However, this pension was due to the fact that she was now considered a widow of a war veteran and not due to her own contributions to the US military. It was a godsend to have a stable income of any kind; however, even this meager penance wasn't easy for Harriet to come by.

There appears to have been a mix-up as to who her husband really was. This stems from the fact that the man Harriet married by the name of Nelson Davis was actually called Nelson Charles when he was a slave (it is believed that he became a runaway slave in 1861). When he served in the Civil War, he was registered as Nelson Charles. It was only after the war and the Emancipation Proclamation that Nelson—like many other former slaves at the time—chose to change his name.

So, by the time of his marriage to Harriet, he was going by the name of Nelson Davis. In order to prove the veracity of her claims, Harriet had to provide documentation to prove that the same Nelson Charles, who was listed as being part of the 8th United States Colored Infantry Regiment in the Civil War, was the same man that she married.

It was a struggle, but Harriet was ultimately able to prove her case well enough to receive a monthly allotment of eight dollars for her widow's pension, which she began receiving for the rest of her life. It may not seem like much, but for Harriet, who had bounced around from job to job all of her life, this small pension was the most stable form of income she had ever had. Eight dollars, of course, also went a lot further in the 1890s than it does today. This monthly allotment was at least enough to allow her to buy her monthly groceries so that she could feed the growing list of family and friends that depended upon her.

Harriet had left the spotlight for a while, but by the time Harriet was in her late sixties, she once again became a public figure for equality, for it was at this time that she began to give speeches for the growing women's rights movement. She actually joined up with the National American Woman Suffrage Association (NAWSA), joining the ranks with the likes of Elizabeth Cady Stanton, Susan B. Anthony, and Emily Howland.

Part of the impetus to get involved with the women's rights movement was the fact that in 1870, even though African American men were given the right to vote, women—whether they were black or white—had not yet been given that privilege. Harriet, no doubt, thought it to be absurd that someone like her who had struggled and fought so hard for her country was not allowed to take part in the electoral process.

Harriet would soon become a regular contributor to the women's suffrage movement, attending gatherings in New York, Boston,

Washington, DC, and the like. She captivated audiences by retelling her stories of working the Underground Railroad and her service during the Civil War. As captivating as these accounts were, they weren't just for entertainment value: they were to drive home the point that strong and determined women can do great things if they simply put their mind to it.

At one of these events, Harriet made an especially strong case for this, and she once recounted her service during the Civil War and how she bore witness to ladies that "were on the scene to administer to the injured, to bind up their wounds and tend them through weary months of suffering in army hospitals." Right when she had the audience's attention, she then posed the question, "If those deeds do not place woman as man's equal, what do?"

Unfortunately, women would not get the right to vote until 1920, a full seven years after Harriet Tubman had already passed away. Nevertheless, she knew that the women's movement was on the right track, and with enough momentum, they would one day prevail. Sadly, the unity of the women's movement would not always hold up due to the racial sensibilities of the day, and Harriet, at times, found herself shut out.

On at least one occasion, while she was in town for a women's conference, she could not find a hotel that would allow her to stay in it—for no other reason than the color of her skin. She would later admit to her friends that she ended up sleeping at a train station just prior to the meeting. Horrified that Harriet would have to sleep out in public like this, her friends then made sure that one of them made arrangements for her to stay with them prior to any future conferences.

In the summer of 1896, Harriet also began speaking at meetings for the National Association of Colored Women's Clubs (NACWC). She actually spoke at their very first meeting, which was held in July of that year, at a special conference in Washington, DC. It's said that before she spoke, the conference held a special "tribute" to Tubman, showing a "picture of her holding a shotgun," with Harriet being praised—among other things—as a "Black Joan of Arc" leading her people to freedom.

Another pet project of hers during this time was the establishment of a shelter for homeless, poor, and disabled African Americans. It was in furtherance of this cause that Harriet went to a public auction in Auburn in 1896 and secured a 25-acre piece of property with a winning bid of $1,450. She then reached out to the local African Methodist Episcopal Zion Church and had them agree to assist her with getting a mortgage from the bank for one thousand dollars. Soon thereafter, the African Methodist reverend, G. C. Carter, became interested in the project and managed to raise enough funds for Tubman to start operations.

Another positive side effect of Tubman's name being mentioned again in the public circles of Auburn was that people began to talk once more about the "shame" of Tubman not receiving compensation for her service during the Civil War. At this point, she was only receiving a widow's pension for her deceased husband, but she was still not receiving a pension for her own service during the war. An article published in 1896 made mention of this fact. "It seems strange that one who has done so much for her country and been in the thick of the battles with shots falling all about her, should never have had recognition from the Government in a substantial way."

Republican politicians at this time were still highly supportive of Civil War veterans in general and the rights of disenfranchised African Americans in particular. Soon, a Republican congressman from New York, by the name of Sereno E. Payne, became determined to "bring up the matter again [of Harriet's pension] and press it to a final and successful termination." Congressman Payne did indeed manage to bring the matter to the attention of the Committee on Invalid Pensions. The petition to the committee did not make any mention of backpay; instead, it just made the basic claim that Tubman should be getting a regular monthly "military pension" amounting to $25 a month.

There was trouble with the documentation of Harriet's service, however, and the members had great difficulty in finding any official mention of her in the record. The best that the committee could come up with was that Harriet might have "been a confidential agent of the Department of State or of Secretary Seward, rather than of the War Department." But, at the same time, this concession came with a warning: "The records which we have received from the Department of State contain no reference to her."

The fact that Harriet—the famed conductor of the Underground Railroad—did her work under the radar should be of no surprise to anyone. Ever since she had fled slavery, she lived and worked under assumed names and rarely documented anything she did. Still, this lack of her name in the official record was a stalling point for those—such as Southern Democrats—who wished to keep Harriet from receiving a pension.

Nevertheless, a determination was eventually made, and although Tubman was not going to be given a military pension under her name, it was determined that in light of the evidence of the services that she had rendered, she would receive a generous increase in the widow's pension she was already receiving. This meant that her previous pension of eight dollars would be increased to twenty dollars.

In light of recent plans of putting Harriet Tubman's likeness on the twenty-dollar bill, many have noted the irony that she would live off twenty dollars a month in the last years of her life. At any rate, this matter was a done deal, and it was signed off on by none other than President William McKinley himself in February of 1899.

It is perhaps fitting that it was McKinley who signed off on it, as he himself served in the Civil War. McKinley, who began his presidency in 1897, was in his fifties when he was sworn into office. Several decades prior, he was a young Union soldier assigned to Company E of the 23rd Ohio Infantry. He was a dedicated soldier who was quickly promoted to sergeant.

McKinley ended up being part of the charge in the Battle of Antietam, which forced Confederate General Robert E. Lee and his men to make a run for it. During the carnage that ensued, McKinley, the great multitasker that he was, stocked up a whole carriage full of food and rushed it to the troops on the front lines, all while dodging enemy artillery blasts. For this incredible feat, he was given yet another promotion—this time to lieutenant. Before the war was over, he would be promoted yet again, becoming a brevet major.

After the war came to a close, McKinley had a mixed record when it came to civil rights. He was personally ambitious when it came to equality and had seen to it that several African Americans were appointed to federal office. He famously appointed Walter L. Cohen from the so-called Black and Tan Republicans as a customs inspector, as well as an African American man by the name of George B. Jackson as a customs collector.

At the same time, however, many accused McKinley of turning a deaf ear to some of the abuses that were going on against African Americans in the South, as the Jim Crow laws that were enacted there only served to enforce racial segregation. And even worse, when the Supreme Court reached its infamous "separate but equal" verdict in the Plessy v. Ferguson case, which all but enshrined segregation in the South, McKinley didn't dare rock the boat. Since he was afraid of losing votes from an "alienated Southern electorate," he refrained from using the bully pulpit of the presidency to address the matter.

It's not clear if he knew of Harriet Tubman's exploits while he served in the war, but he most certainly would have heard of them afterward. And despite his dithering on key civil rights issues, he always made it clear how much he valued the valiant efforts of African Americans like Tubman in their pursuit of freedom. As McKinley himself once put it, "Our black allies must neither be forsaken nor deserted. I weigh my words. This is the great question not only of the present, but is the great question of the future; and this question will never be settled until it is settled upon the principles of justice, recognizing the sanctity of the Constitution of the United States."

So, if his words can be any judge of his character, and excluding the political expediencies of the day, it would seem that his heart was at least in the right place. As such, by the time the request to raise Harriet Tubman's pension came to his desk, he didn't hesitate to sign off on it.

Harriet, in the meantime, had managed to receive some pretty admirable recognition from even farther abroad, as she was invited to England for none other than Queen Victoria's 1897 birthday celebration. Victoria had apparently read the biography of Tubman and was impressed by her exploits. Tubman was flattered at the invitation, but considering her meager finances, she was unable to make the trip.

Nevertheless, the queen showed her magnanimity by sending Harriet a silver medal that had the "likenesses of Queen Victoria, her son, grandson, and great grandson" on it. The queen also sent her a silk shawl to go along with it. These were items that Harriet would hold dear for the rest of her life. In one of her most famous photos, which was taken near the end of her life, she can be seen relaxing in a chair, wearing that very shawl.

It was a great honor to receive such recognition from the queen of England. Despite the obvious thrill of being taken into consideration by such a notable personage, in many ways, the queen of England was a symbol of the Underground Railroad itself. How could this be? Decades before the United States issued the Emancipation Proclamation to free America's slaves, Britain had already ended slavery all throughout its empire. And during Harriet Tubman's heyday of leading slaves to freedom on the Underground Railroad, Canada, the British territory to the north, represented the safest place a runaway could go.

In 1850, though, once the Fugitive Slave Act was passed, even the Northern states were no longer safe havens. It was for this reason that Tubman and other conductors of the Underground Railroad ultimately looked toward Canada as their safest bet for freedom. As Harriet herself once put it, "I wouldn't trust Uncle Sam with my people no longer, but I brought 'em all clear off to Canada." So it was that the queen of England had come to represent a kind of "symbol of freedom," and it must have been very exciting for Harriet to receive this courtesy from her.

Along with such boosts to her self-esteem, Tubman's increase in her pension helped her out tremendously, enabling her to not have to work odd jobs just to survive. This not only gave her worn-out body a much-deserved rest, but it also gave her more free time to focus on her philanthropic endeavors and social activism. It may have even given her the opportunity to have brain surgery.

Although it is not known for sure the exact details, like many of the other murkier aspects of Harriet Tubman's life, it is widely believed that it was around this time that Harriet finally sought treatment for the head injury that had plagued her for most of her life. Ever since she was struck in the forehead with a two-pound weight as a little girl, she had suffered repeated headaches, sleep disturbances, and even seizures. She would, at times, attribute her visionary experiences to this injury, so, in her mind, it was both a blessing and a curse.

But by this stage in life, the headaches had become just about unbearable. Seeking relief, it's said that she checked into Massachusetts General Hospital and had a doctor operate on her brain. According to legend, she supposedly refused anesthesia and simply requested to have a bullet placed between her clenched teeth instead. This was apparently in imitation of the Civil War soldiers who suffered through similar pain during the war. Many biographers are doubtful of this part of the story, as it is now widely known that Tubman did tend to exaggerate some details of her life. But nevertheless, she apparently did have some sort of operation to alleviate some of the pain that she had been experiencing.

The late 1890s brought us another memorable milestone in the life of Harriet Tubman when she was interviewed by Wilbur H. Siebert, the celebrated writer of the 1898 classic, *The Underground Railroad from Slavery to Freedom*. Siebert spent quite a bit of time speaking with Harriet Tubman, and he always left every discussion he had with her in complete awe of who it was that he was speaking with.

Siebert praised Harriet Tubman as one who "saw in the oppression of her race the sufferings of the enslaved Israelites, and was not slow to demand that the pharaoh of the South should let her people go." Siebert, like many, recognized in the wizened features of Harriet Tubman a true leader, someone who was willing to sacrifice everything in order to lift up the downtrodden and the oppressed.

Harriet was as strong-willed as ever, but as she approached eighty years old, she was becoming less able to handle the running of her multiple properties. Feeling burdened and overwhelmed by the upkeep, in 1903, she decided to donate the extra property that she had purchased to the African Methodist Episcopal Zion Church.

Harriet Tubman, meanwhile, now free from this excess burden, took the time to once again attend meetings and conferences for liberal causes. Most notably during this period, she appeared before an audience with Susan B. Anthony at a gathering of the New York State Woman Suffrage Association in 1904.

It was a few years after this that the African Methodist Episcopal Zion Church would use the property Harriet donated to open up the Harriet Tubman Home for the Aged in 1908. Tubman herself was there as a special guest of honor for the event. The day is said to have been a mixture of "parade, prayers, and speeches," along with a musical performance, dinner, and dancing, with Harriet seated with an American flag draped about her shoulders at the center of it all. One of the local papers made mention of this occasion, stating:

> With the Stars and Stripes wound about her shoulders, a band playing national airs and a concourse of members of her race gathered about her to pay tribute to her lifelong struggle on behalf of the colored people of America, aged Harriet Tubman Davis, the Moses of her race, yesterday experienced one of the happiest moments of her life, a period to which she has looked forward for a score of years. The Harriet Tubman Home is today an accomplished fact.

Interestingly enough, Harriet herself would become a resident of this very institution that she helped to establish. Tubman began living in the home in 1911, and one of her most memorable interviews occurred during this period when she was questioned by James B. Clarke, a student from Cornell University, who had already become famous for his activism on campus against discrimination.

Clarke was greatly impressed with Harriet Tubman, saying that despite being in her golden years, she was still "astonishingly fresh and active." He recalled her "coming downstairs to breakfast" and having a "hearty meal" of "spring chicken with rice, pie, cheese, and other good things." He later wrote that the spry Harriet Tubman "resented the notion" that her nurse sometimes attempted to "feed her," insisting that she could take care of herself.

She also impressed Clarke with her ability to regale him with all manner of reinvented tales about her life. She was proud of the things she had done and all of the famous people that she had met along the way. This was evidenced when she pulled out the medal given to her by Britain's Queen Victoria, showing just how much she appreciated these important connections in her life. But above all, Clarke was impressed with her testimony of how she encouraged the deliverance of so many from the bonds of slavery. As Clarke put it, "Her life has been one long 'word of consolation' and an inspiration to her people."

Besides the occasional visits from admirers such as this, most of Tubman's last days were spent in quiet reflection in the nursing home that she herself helped found. She would live at the Harriet Tubman Home for the Aged from 1911 until the day she died on March 10th, 1913. Although she may have been energetic and talkative when interviewed by James B. Clarke, soon after, she all but lost the pep in her step.

In the end, the great conductor, stricken with a bad case of pneumonia, found herself unable to get out of her bed. Nevertheless, when she passed away at 91 years of age, it is said that her last words were, "I go to prepare a place for you." Incredibly enough, as much as she led the way in this life, with her final statement, she seemed to indicate that she was ready to lead the way in the next life as well.

After her funeral service, Harriet Tubman was laid to rest at Fort Hill Cemetery in Auburn, New York. It was a grand affair, with Tubman being honored as if she had once been a head of state. She was buried with Queen Victoria's medal around her neck and an American flag draped over her coffin.

The papers all mentioned Tubman's passing with printed articles such as the one that appeared in *The Washington Herald*, which proclaimed, "Colored Moses of Her People Dies in the Home She Founded." Such headlines are captivating yet sublime at the same time. Such a title seems to suggest that this great figure, while being the larger than life "Moses of her people," had proven herself to be mortal just like all of the rest of us, passing away in the very home she founded.

But beyond the newspaper headlines, we are perhaps best keyed into the enormity of this event by way of a photo taken on the day of Harriet's funeral service, which showed the huge throng of mourners (African American and European American alike) gathered around her coffin. The fact that the citizens of Auburn, New York, were so supportive was a clear demonstration of just how important a fixture Tubman was to her friends and neighbors.

In the days following her death, the people of Auburn wanted to do more for her memory, and so, they raised money to install a special commemorative plaque bearing her name on the grounds of the Cayuga County Courthouse. This plaque read, in part, "In Memory of Harriet Tubman. Born a slave in Maryland about 1821 [although many now say 1820]. Died in Auburn, N.Y. March 10th, 1913. Called the 'Moses' of her people during the Civil War, with rare courage she led over 300 negroes up from slavery to freedom. And rendered invaluable service as a nurse and spy. With implicit trust in God, she braved every danger and overcame every obstacle."

At the plaque's unveiling in 1914, prominent African American leader Booker T. Washington was present, among others. Booker gave a stirring speech in which he described Harriet as a powerful role model while also promoting his current work for the African American community through his Tuskegee Institute.

As for the Tubman Home? It would carry on without its namesake over the next couple of decades, but ultimately, it would go out of business. The property itself was nearly lost in the 1940s due to back taxes, but the African Methodist Episcopal Zion Church managed to raise enough funds to retain the land. They were then able to renovate parts of the property and have since turned it into a museum, which is run by the church.

The museum has been a constant draw for anyone passing through the area. All are eager to retrace the steps of this brave lady who blazed her own rich and exciting path in life. Her last words, after all, were, "I prepare a place for you." And anyone whose hearts have been touched by her powerful story would most certainly agree that history has most certainly prepared a place for her.

Conclusion: The Leading Light of Freedom

Harriet Tubman was no doubt the most successful conductor the Underground Railroad had ever known. Although the exact number is not known and the fact that many of her exploits are brought to us through a series of often disjointed anecdotal tales, it is believed that Tubman may have led as many as three hundred souls to freedom. At times, it seemed that even Harriet Tubman herself couldn't quite remember all of the places she had visited and the people that she had brought forth.

Tubman may not have been the originator of the Underground Railroad, but she most certainly made the most of it. Anyone could have made use of the trails and safe houses that the Underground Railroad had established, but few did. It took someone with real courage and ambition to get out there and do it. Harriet Tubman had that ambition.

Even when her own brothers decided to turn back, preferring the known hardship of slavery to the unknown, Harriet forged ahead. Unlike them, she didn't spend time worrying about what might happen if she was caught, what might happen if she got lost, what might happen if she starved. Instead of thinking about what might happen in the future, Harriet Tubman was mindful of the moment. She literally took her journey one step at a time.

Besides her accomplishments as a conductor on the Underground Railroad, it was her service for the Union Army of which she was always the proudest. She truly cherished the time she spent as a nurse caring for the troops, as well as her work gathering intelligence for the Union advance.

But probably her most memorable moment was when she led that infamous raid down the Combahee River in June of 1863. Here, Harriet Tubman, in a very real sense, served as a beacon of hope in the midst of those who were still in bondage. As she stood tall on the decks of those gunboats as they traveled downriver, countless slaves that had long feared being "sold down the river" were eagerly hopping right aboard.

For they knew that with Harriet there in their midst, it was "okay." They knew that as long as Harriet was at the helm, they had nothing to fear and that they would come to no harm. Harriet Tubman herself often said—and it's worth repeating again—that in all the missions she undertook for liberty, for all who agreed to follow her through the wilderness, she never once left anyone behind.

And she was always quick to tell anyone who would listen, "I was the conductor of the Underground Railroad for eight years, and I can say what most conductors can't say—I never ran my train off the track and I never lost a passenger." She was indeed the good and able steward, and just as she led her passengers to freedom in the past, she is still the leading light of freedom to this very day.

Appendix A: Reading and Reference

Harriet Tubman for Beginners. Annette Alson.

Harriet Tubman: Freedom Seeker, Freedom Leader. Rosemary Sadlier.

Harriet Tubman: Abolitionist and Conductor of the Underground Railroad. Barbara Krasner and Heather Moore Niver.

Harriet: The Moses of her People. Sarah H. Bradford.

Harriet Tubman: Conductor on the Underground Railroad. Ann Petry.

Harriet Tubman: The Life and the Life Stories. Jean McMahon Humez.

Conjuring Harriet "Mama Moses" Tubman: And the Spirits of the Underground Railroad. Witchdoctor Utu.

Harriet Tubman: Myth, Memory and History. Milton C. Sernett.

Harriet Tubman: Imagining a Life. Beverly Lowry.

She Came to Slay: The Life and Times of Harriet Tubman. Erica Armstrong Dunbar.

Harriet Tubman: The Road to Freedom. Catherine Clinton.

John Brown, Abolitionist: The Man Who Killed Slavery, Sparked the Civil War, and Seeded Civil Rights. David S. Reynolds.

The Abolition of Slavery. Diane Yancey.

Free Bonus from Captivating History (Available for a Limited time)

Hi History Lovers!

Now you have a chance to join our exclusive history list so you can get your first history ebook for free as well as discounts and a potential to get more history books for free! Simply visit the link below to join.

Captivatinghistory.com/ebook

Also, make sure to follow us on Facebook, Twitter and Youtube by searching for Captivating History.

**Here's another book by Captivating History
that you might be interested in**

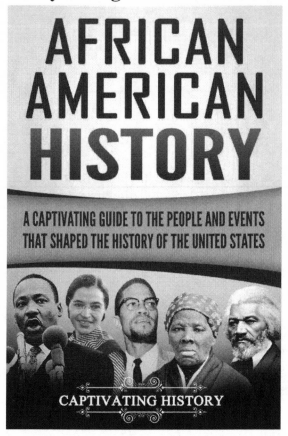